Plants of Indiana

and Adjacent States

Alan McPherson

and Sue McPherson

Indiana University Press
BLOOMINGTON & LONDON

Published in Canada by Fitzhenry & Whiteside Limited, Don Mills,
Ontario

Manufactured in the United States of America

Library of Congress Cataloging in Publication Data
McPherson, Alan, 1947–
Wild food plants of Indiana and adjacent states.
Bibliography
Includes index.
1. Wild plants, Edible—Indiana—Identification.
I. McPherson, Sue, 1948–   joint author. II. Title.
QK98.5.U6M3   581.6′32′09772   76–48528
ISBN 0–253–19039–8
ISBN 0–253–28925–4 pbk.   1 2 3 4 5 81 80 79 78 77

Contents

ACKNOWLEDGMENTS

We wish to express our gratitude to the many people who have helped and guided us in the preparation of this book. We wish to thank our families for their endless encouragement and boundless love. We are indebted to John Brooks for his many imaginative drawings. We are grateful to Indiana University Press for giving us the opportunity to make this book a reality. We appreciate the enthusiasm of our friends who willingly tasted our wild food creations and offered suggestions as well as praise. Finally, we would like to thank all the Hoosiers who shared with us their own wild food foraging experience.

Wild Food Plants
of Indiana
and Adjacent States

*I am singularly refreshed in winter when I
hear of service-berries, poke-weed, juniper.
Is not heaven made up of these cheap
summer glories?*
HENRY DAVID THOREAU

A Plant
Perspective of Indiana

Thanks largely to the late Euell Gibbons (whose "stalking" books deserve a prized place on every wild food plant forager's bookshelf), interest in gathering edible wild plants has never been greater. But plants vary considerably from one region to the next. To the best of our knowledge this is the first guide to wild food plants tailored specifically to the needs of Hoosiers and their neighbors.

Hoosiers are fortunate; Indiana offers a wide variety of plant habitats and it is the meeting ground of plant migrations from all directions. Prairie plants from the west, Atlantic coastal plants from the east, arctic plants from the north, and Appalachian, lower Mississipian, and Gulf region plants from the south—members of all these plant communities have found their way into Indiana and are at home here. This botanical wealth is the result of the varying topographies, climates, and soils the state possesses. In respect to climate, Indiana is a plant crossroads, or transitional zone, since nearly half of the species found in the state are at one limit of their range here. The pecan, a southern tree, reaches its northeasternmost limit in Indiana and the jack pine, a northern tree, reaches its southernmost limit here. Other species reach their eastern or western limits.

Until recently, little consideration was given to Hoosier plant communities except by specialists. But in order to be a really good wild food forager, it is important to come to a basic understanding of the plant communities of Indiana. We have divided the state into eight natural areas. Our simplified interpretation is derived from *Flora of Indiana* by Charles Deam and *Natural Areas in Indiana and Their Preservation* by A. A. Lindsey, D. V. Schmelz, and S. A. Nichols. Botanically Indiana is more complex than our eight divisions would make it appear. However, this simplified interpretation will give the wild food forager a plant perspective of Indiana. The eight natural areas are the Dunes, the Lake Area, the Prairie, the Tipton Till Plain, the Lower Wabash Valley, the Southwestern Lowlands, the South-Central Mixed Woods, and the Southeastern Till Plain.

Each of the eight areas supports its own distinctive plant communities. A great and, for the most part, destructive influence on present-day plant communities has been the impact of man on his environment. The arrival of European settlers and the subsequent invention of the steel plow changed Indiana radically. Many plant species vanished as the earth was harnessed for agriculture. Today we have a state much-altered from the one first encountered by our ancestors; thus, many of the plant communities are only sad remnants of their former bounty.

The Dunes follow the southern border of Lake Michigan. This area is composed of high and low dunes, sloughs, and interdunal flats. Dunes, which are ridges of windblown sand, are generally common features of deserts and seacoasts but

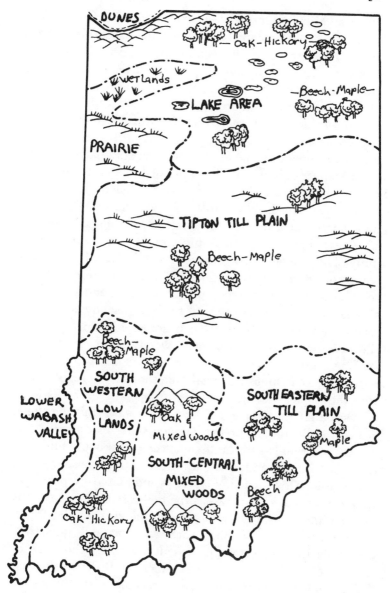

the Lake Michigan area is not arid, neither is it a seacoast. As early as 1890 botanists realized how exceptional the Indiana Dunes are. Since the Dunes offer a perfect opportunity to study plant succession, steps were taken to protect this unique area. For this reason, the Dunes are considered the birthplace of American ecology. Nevertheless, the Dunes are situated in one of the most highly industrialized regions in the world and man's encroachment is still a threat to the precarious life of the dunes. Much of the flora of the Dunes is unique and exists in no other part of Indiana, for example, bunchberry, Bailey dogwood, and beach pea. Entire books have been devoted to Dunes vegetation. The vegetation varies according to the changes in the exposure and steepness of the slopes. Jack pine reaches the southernmost limit of its range in the Dunes. Farther inland, black and white oaks dominate the drier dunal areas. The forest floor is covered with huckleberry and bracken fern, and its borders abound in sumac and butternut as well as sand cherries and juneberries. Nearer the water is beach grass, which provides stability for the establishment of woody plants in the ever-shifting sand.

The Indiana Dunes National Lakeshore was created to insure that at least some part of this special region would be preserved for the people and for its own sake. But the Dunes are very delicate. The precarious sands are seldom still. Constantly rearranging the landscape, the continuous shifting of the sand buries and unburies trees, often revealing tree graveyards. This unsteady world is inundated by people as well as by sand—the park has the highest attendance of any Indiana state park. Only by thoughtful use can the Dunes survive. Stay on paths and protect the unstable sand from wind erosion. Do not forage without a permit, which can be picked up at the Visitor Center. Abuse will diminish what little remains of this unique area. Remember, the Dunes are fragile; handle with care.

Below the dunal area, the Lake Area occupies the north-eastern and extreme northwestern part of the state. Within this area, three hundred species of plants reach their southernmost limit. Examples are tamarack trees, sundews, starflowers, and bog orchids. This once much-glaciated area is characterized by a wide variety of habitats including lakes, rivers, bogs, and marshes, as well as dry sand and gravelly places. Because of extensive draining and filling, many of the marshes have disappeared and given way to plains that are more suitable for agriculture. More lakes have been destroyed in Indiana than exist today. Olin Lake Preserve in LaGrange County is the largest remaining undeveloped natural lake in the state. This 120-acre area is a remnant of the last glacial period and is considered to be the cleanest lake in Indiana. Drainage lowered the water level of many lakes, creating bogs and swamps. Marl deposits and plant deposition dried up a large number of the lakes. Such wild food plants as arrowheads, cattails, water lilies, and bulrushes are at home in these lakes and marshes. The Lake Area also has occasional patches of prairie and oak openings. Oak openings are groves of bur oaks that were once scattered throughout the sea of prairie grass. The thick, corky bark of old bur oaks gave these trees an armor that could withstand the periodic spontaneous prairie fires. With the bur oaks there were sometimes hickories and walnuts as well as other types of oaks but understory growth was sparse, except for grasses, since the soil was usually sandy.

West of the Lake Area and south of the Dunes lies the irregular boundary of the small Prairie Area. The Prairie Area was once a grassland interspersed with oaks that gave the landscape a savannalike appearance. There were wet prairie areas and dry prairie areas as well as the areas where grassland and forest met. The greater part of the prairie was wet prairie, which had water at or near the surface of the ground during part of the year. In the wet prairie little bluestem predominated although Indian grass and reed grass were also common. The dry prairie areas were excessively drained and were characterized by big bluestem. Both areas abounded with asters and goldenrods. Besides these, compass plants, prairie clovers, and prairie sunflowers were common. The prairie border trees were mostly white, black, bur, and jack oak.

Cool-season prairie plants such as Canada wild rye and Pennsylvania sedge began growing very early in the spring and were mature by early summer. Warm-season species such as big and little bluestem, Indian grass, and prairie dropseed didn't begin to grow until the weather was warmer but their growing season extended into late summer and early fall. The combination of cool-season species and warm-season species provided a continuous food supply for birds and other animals.

Thirteen percent of the Indiana landscape was prairie until 1840 when the steel plow, which was strong enough to penetrate the hard prairie soil, was developed. Now there are few areas not under the plow, and a great majority of prairie flora have been destroyed. Many prairie wildflowers could not withstand the onslaught of farms, towns, and trampling livestock. The prairie grasses disappeared, to be replaced by corn and soybeans. The prairie chicken disappeared along with his prairie. The best variety of typical prairie flora is preserved in the Jasper-Pulaski State Fish and Wildlife Area. An assortment of the few prairie plants that remain in the wild can be seen along roadsides and railroad right-of-ways, in waste places, and, especially, in old cemeteries.

South of the Wabash River lies the level Tipton Till Plain of central Indiana. This flat to gently rippling plain has scattered low ridges and lone hills or groups of hills. There is only slight variation in the topography. Since the soil is mostly neutral or only slightly acid, the acid-loving plants of the north and south are absent in this area. Plants from all directions reach their limits of distribution in this broad, central plain. The Tipton Till Plain was once covered with beech–maple forests but since some of the best agricultural land in Indiana is found here, nearly all of the woodlands have disappeared. This entire area has little of the original flora and fauna left. Miles and miles of trees have been replaced by miles and miles of corn and soybeans. The scattered woods that do remain are well cut over; they usually contain an understory of greenbriar, pawpaw, spicebush, and elderberry. Mayapple, false Solomon's seal, wild ginger, and jack-in-the-pulpit are other features of these scattered beech–maple woods. Along Sugar Creek in Turkey Run State Park, very large trees that are remnants of floodplain forests can still be seen.

The Lower Wabash Valley is a narrow strip of land along the Wabash River from Vigo County south to the Ohio. Many plants associated with the Lower Mississippi Valley, such as the bald cypress, are found here. The Little Cypress Swamp in Knox County and the Cypress Slough in Posey County are the best examples of cypress swamps. In 1874, 20,000 acres in the southwestern part of Knox County were covered with cypress. Today about 360 acres are all that remain. The cypress is a slow-growing member of the Pine Family. Like the tamarack, another member of the Pine Family, cypresses shed their needles every year. The cypress trees bear cone-like fruit. Their wet habitat causes "knees" to develop from the roots and project above the water level and the trunks swell at the base, giving the trees a strange appearance. The understory of the Little Cypress Swamp is buttonbush and spicebush mingled with dense clumps of southern cane. The Cypress Slough in Posey County covers 120 acres and is the most extensive stand of large cypress trees in Indiana. Besides the cypress you can find pecan, big shellbark hickory, honey locust, sugarberry, and Shumard's red oak. The Lower

Wabash Valley is more closely associated with the Mississippi Valley than any other area in Indiana. Cypress, pecan, sugarberry, and overcup oak reach their northern limit in the Lower Wabash Valley. Some other plants at their northern limit are woolly pipe-vine, indigo bush, Texas adelia, and Carolina snailseed.

Adjacent to the Lower Wabash Valley is the glaciated area of the Southwestern Lowlands. The lowlands are usually wooded with pin oaks and shingle oaks. In the northwestern part of Daviess County there are dunes and in the low spots between the dunes live many plants associated with the Atlantic Coastal Plain. There are a number of sandy terraces such as the terrace of the Wabash River, which begins north of Terre Haute and extends southwards to Posey County. These sandy terraces, results of glacial sand deposits, are raised banks of sand with sloping sides and flat tops; on them grow many plants, such as indigo bush and southern cane, that are associated with the Lower Mississippi Valley.

In the unglaciated section of the South-Central Mixed Woods numerous southern plants reach their northern limit of distribution. The eastern section of this region is hilly and wooded. There is an abundance of oaks, especially chestnut oaks, and before the chestnut blight, the American chestnut was abundant here. On the many high ridges or knobs, pawpaw, spicebush, and greenbriar are common. The flora of these knobs is quite diversified; often the north side of a knob will have plants at their southern limit while the south side will have plants at their northern limit. Donaldson's Woods in Spring Mill State Park is considered the best remaining stand of virgin woods in the area. This woods is mainly white oak, sugar maple, and beech. The western section of the South-Central Mixed Woods is gently sloping with low hills and high ground. The high woods are primarily beech, tulip, and sugar maple. The low land has oak, hickory, elm, and sweet gum.

The glaciated Southeastern Till Plain has a number of flats; these are level, poorly drained areas with acid soil. High flats support beech, tulip, sweet gum, and black gum trees. In the low flats, swamp chestnut oak, swamp white oak, pin oak, southern red oak, and red maple can be found. Not all of these trees will exist in any one area; instead only two or three species will dominate. The buckeye and white basswood found here are commonly associated with forests farther south. Versailles State Park in Ripley County and Muscatatuck National Wildlife Refuge in Jackson County are areas that are excellent representatives of the Southeastern Till Plain topography.

As you can see, Indiana is a land of diversity; and the forager has a wide variety of plants to choose from. Knowing where to look for certain plants is helpful. Some wild food plants are found only in one natural area; many are found in all eight natural areas. However, in all eight divisions there are very few areas that have not been disrupted by man. Settlers often knowingly, sometimes accidentally, introduced plants into the New World. Sometimes these migrant plants were welcomed but all too often they came to seem more like foreign invaders. Farmers still battle the Canadian thistle, which was introduced from Europe. Every year lives are lost to poison hemlock, a native of Europe that has spread through North America. On the other hand, wild food foragers enjoy such immigrants as chickweed, dandelion, and day lilies.

Man's intervention dealt deathblows to some species but gave life to many plants sought after by wild food hunters. Most wild food plants do not do well in deep forests. When man denuded an area certain species such as elderberry, lamb's quarters, and milkweed were quick to recover. Raspberries, blackberries, and roses rushed to form thickets in vacant areas. Sun-loving plants such as the Jerusalem artichoke relished the clearings men created. Smaller trees such as mulberry, wild cherry, crab apple, and hawthorn soon became established. Nevertheless, the abundance of one plant often means the loss of another. Many plants cannot adapt to the encroachment of civilization. Draining the wetlands, leveling the forests, and plowing up the prairies have taken their toll. Before white men settled Indiana, plants such as the American lotus were abundant but drainage and thoughtless foraging have all but eradicated this beautiful, edible plant.

We hope that the wild food forager using this book will be ecologically minded as he forages. Gather only what you need and will use. Do not gather rare or endangered plants. (Generally we have not included in this book plants that we feel are too rare to encourage foraging.) Please use good judgment on what and how much you forage. Never take the entire stand of any wild plant since this could endanger the plant's reproduction and could seriously deplete the food supply available for birds, deer, and other wildlife. The Indians understood the balance of nature and lived within its harmony; they maintained the ecological balance because they revered the plants that sustained their lives. The modern wild food hunter will seldom, if ever, be foraging for survival. There is no reason to endanger the existence of any species.

The greatest challenge in wild food hunting is correct identification of the plant. There is no general rule for telling whether a plant is poisonous. Day lilies have edible flowers and bulbs but wild iris has flowers and bulbs that are poisonous. The only safe way to determine if a plant is edible is to identify the plant. If in doubt, don't eat it. Indians tested the edibility of plants by feeding the plants to captives from other tribes. If they did not become ill, obviously the plant was edible. However, present-day foragers will have to rely on plant descriptions and pictures. Of course, the ideal way to identify a plant is firsthand from a

guide who knows wild foods. We have tried to present our
book in a simple, straightforward style and to describe the
plants carefully. Once you have identified a plant and eaten
it, you will probably not forget it. Most plants will be easily
identifiable, but do remember that accurate identification
is essential. When in doubt, don't eat it.

When foraging you will find it helpful to take along some
plastic bags, a sharp pocketknife, and a folding shovel or
garden trowel. This prevents frustration when you are con-
fronted with lots of plants and have no way to gather them
and no way to carry them.

At the back of this book you will find a list of helpful
books, ones that we have found invaluable in our own pur-
suit of wild foods. The county map of Indiana on page 14
will help you when the distribution of a plant is given by
county. The plant distributions we give are from Charles
Deam's monumental work, *Flora of Indiana,* in which Deam
systematically identifies and catalogs every vascular plant
found in Indiana. Although the botanical jargon is sometimes discouraging to the layman, Deam's book is a useful
resource for anyone interested in Indiana flora and it includes a generous sprinkling of folklore and Hoosier wisdom.

The seasonal guide tells you what wild foods to look for
at a particular time of year. Happy foraging! We think you
will find, as we have, that the greatest satisfaction in knowing plants by name is that they are no longer strangers, but
friends.

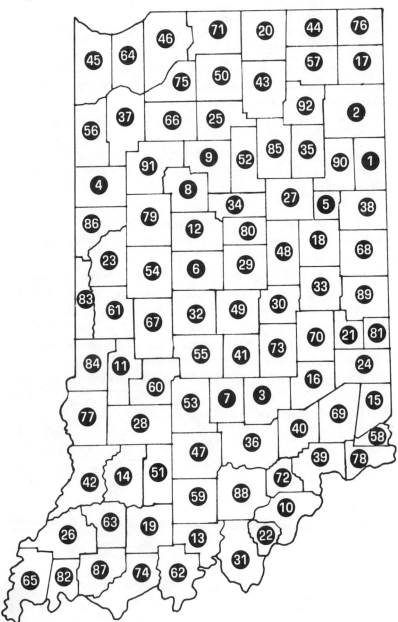

COUNTY MAP OF INDIANA

1	Adams	32	Hendricks	63	Pike
2	Allen	33	Henry	64	Porter
3	Bartholomew	34	Howard	65	Posey
4	Benton	35	Huntington	66	Pulaski
5	Blackford	36	Jackson	67	Putnam
6	Boone	37	Jasper	68	Randolph
7	Brown	38	Jay	69	Ripley
8	Carroll	39	Jefferson	70	Rush
9	Cass	40	Jennings	71	St. Joseph
10	Clark	41	Johnson	72	Scott
11	Clay	42	Knox	73	Shelby
12	Clinton	43	Kosciusko	74	Spencer
13	Crawford	44	LaGrange	75	Starke
14	Daviess	45	Lake	76	Steuben
15	Dearborn	46	LaPorte	77	Sullivan
16	Decatur	47	Lawrence	78	Switzerland
17	De Kalb	48	Madison	79	Tippecanoe
18	Delaware	49	Marion	80	Tipton
19	Dubois	50	Marshall	81	Union
20	Elkhart	51	Martin	82	Vanderburgh
21	Fayette	52	Miami	83	Vermillion
22	Floyd	53	Monroe	84	Vigo
23	Fountain	54	Montgomery	85	Wabash
24	Franklin	55	Morgan	86	Warren
25	Fulton	56	Newton	87	Warrick
26	Gibson	57	Noble	88	Washington
27	Grant	58	Ohio	89	Wayne
28	Greene	59	Orange	90	Wells
29	Hamilton	60	Owen	91	White
30	Hancock	61	Parke	92	Whitley
31	Harrison	62	Perry		

A Seasonal Guide
to Wild Food Plants

SPRING

Alfalfa and clovers (leaves)
Arrowheads (early: tubers)
Asparagus (shoots)
Basswoods (flowers)
Bulrush (early: roots)
  (shoots, sprouts)
Cattails (early: roots)
  (shoots, sprouts, spikes)
Chickweed (leaves)
Chicory (leaves, crowns)
Chufa (early: tubers)
Dandelion (leaves, crowns,
  flowers, roots)
Day lily (shoots, flower buds,
  bulbs)
Dock (leaves)

Evening primrose (leaves,
  shoots, roots)
False Solomon's seal (shoots,
  roots)
Ferns (fiddleheads)
Grapes (tendrils, leaves)
Greenbriar (shoots, roots)
Jerusalem artichoke (early:
  tubers)
Lamb's quarters (leaves)
Milkweed (shoots, young
  leaves)
Mints (leaves)
Morels
Mustards (leaves, flower
  buds)

Nettles (leaves)
Onion, garlic, leek (bulbs)
Pines (needles, bark)
Pokeweed (sprouts)
Puffballs
Purslane (leaves, stems)
Roses (buds, petals)
Sassafras (leaves, roots)
Shaggymane
Skunk cabbage (early: roots)
   (leaves)

Solomon's seal (shoots,
   roots)
Sorrels (leaves)
Spicebush (leaves, twigs,
   bark)
Spring beauty (corms)
Strawberry (late: fruits)
Sugar maple (early: sap)
Violets (leaves, flowers)

SUMMER

Alfalfa and clover (greens
   and flowers)
Asparagus (seeds)
Bulrush (pollen)
Cattails (sprouts, pollen)
Cherries (fruit)
Chickweed (leaves)
Chicory (roots)
Day lily (flowers, bulbs)
Dock (leaves)
Elderberry (flowers, fruits)
False Solomon's seal (ber-
   ries)
Grapes (leaves, fruit)
Hazelnuts (nuts)
Juneberry (fruit)
Lamb's quarters (leaves)
Mayapple (fruit)

Milkweed (flower buds,
   young pods)
Mints (leaves)
Mulberries (fruit)
Mustard (seeds)
Nettles (leaves)
New Jersey tea (leaves)
Onion, garlic, leek (early:
   bulbs)
Pawpaw (fruit)
Persimmon (leaves)
Plum (fruit)
Puffballs
Purslane (leaves, stem)
Raspberry, blackberry, dew-
   berry (fruit)
Roses (petals)
Sorrels (leaves)

Spicebush (leaves, twigs,
   bark, berries)
Strawberry (early: fruit)
Sulphur shelf (late)

Sumac (fruit)
Walnuts (early: immature
   nuts)

FALL

American chestnut (nuts)
Arrowhead (tubers)
Bulrush (roots)
Cattails (roots, shoots)
Chickweed (leaves)
Chufa (tubers)
Crab apple (fruit)
Day lily (bulbs)
Dock (leaves)
Elderberry (fruit)
Evening primrose (early:
   roots)
False Solomon's seal (roots)
Ginger (underground stem)
Grapes (early: leaves, fruit)
Greenbriar (roots)
Hawthorns (fruit)
Hazelnut (nuts)
Hickories (nuts)

Jerusalem artichoke (tubers)
Lamb's quarters (leaves,
   seeds)
Mints (leaves)
Oaks (nuts)
Persimmon (fruit)
Pines (seeds)
Puffballs
Roses (fruit)
Shaggymane
Skunk cabbage (roots)
Solomon's seal (roots)
Sorrels (leaves)
Spicebush (berries)
Sugar maple (fruit)
Sulphur shelf
Sumac (fruit)
Walnuts (nuts)
Wild rice (grain)

WINTER

Cattails (roots)
Pines (bark)
Sugar maple (late: sap)

Cinnamon
fern

Ferns

The fiddleheads make their first appearance in late April or early May. The newborn ferns emerge with the trappings of birth still clinging to them and are so named because they resemble the scrolled top of a fiddle. A few of the most commonly found fiddleheads in Indiana are the young shoots of the bracken fern, the cinnamon fern, the sensitive fern, and the Christmas fern. The bracken fern (*Pteridium aquilinum*) is common in the dry sandy soil of the Lake Area but infrequent throughout the rest of the state, where it is most often found in open areas along the edges of woods. The clawlike fiddleheads are covered with silvery gray hair and uncoil into three leaf sections. The cinnamon fern (*Osmunda cinnamomea*) is found throughout the state in wet alluvial or sandy soil in swampy woods and thickets or along the edges of ponds, lakes, and rivers. Its fiddleheads are quite large and at first they are covered with silvery white hairs, which later turn cinnamon brown as the leaves unfold. The sensitive fern (*Onoclea sensibilis*) is frequent throughout the state in low woodland places, near lakes, and along roadsides. Its pale red fiddleheads are very conspicuous in the spring. The Christmas fern or dagger fern (*Polystichum acrostichoides*), which resembles the Boston fern houseplant, is common in wet woods throughout southern Indiana. In protected places the foliage stays green all year. In early spring the Christmas fern produces a profusion of stout, scaly fiddleheads covered with silvery gray hairs.

One early May day while camping in southern Indiana we feasted on fiddleheads found along a small stream in Hoosier National Forest. We chose young fiddleheads not more than six to eight inches high, breaking them off as low as they remained tender and washing off the woolly hairs. Since wild leeks were equally abundant, we put fiddleheads and washed leeks in a skillet with heated oil and sautéed them uncovered for 10 minutes, then added just enough water to steam and a vegetable bouillon cube, and covered them with a lid until they were tender. The vegetables were served over brown rice and topped with sunflower seeds and cheese cubes. It was a feast to remember. Camp meals are certainly enhanced by the addition of fresh, wild foods. Many people eat fiddleheads raw as a nibble but we prefer them cooked. Any recipe for asparagus may be adapted for fiddleheads.

Fiddleheads in wine sauce are delicious served over whole wheat spaghetti. To prepare the sauce, melt ⅓ cup butter in a heavy skillet. Add 1 cup sliced mushrooms and sauté until soft. Over low heat blend in 3 tablespoons flour and cook for 2–4 minutes. Slowly add 2 cups milk and stir with a wooden spoon or wire whisk until the sauce begins to thicken. Add ½ cup red wine and 1½ cups steamed fiddleheads. Continue cooking the sauce until it is creamy and thick. This sauce is equally good served over rice or whole wheat toast.

A note of warning: Although all fiddleheads are edible, they must be young and fresh; the eating of old fiddleheads or the mature ferns has been known to cause poisoning in livestock.

White pine

Pine Family

Although native pines have never been abundant in Indiana, we do have three that are native. The most common native pine is white pine (*Pinus strobus*), which is found in the limited area of the Dunes and the Sugar Creek area. Native scrub pine (*Pinus virginiana*) is found near the Ohio River in Floyd, Clark, and Scott counties. The third native pine is jack pine (*P. banksiana*), which is found only on the dunes of Lake Michigan and is at its southernmost limit in Indiana. Most of the pines we see have been introduced as windbreaks along fencerows and as ornamentals in yards.

A delicious tea can be made from any pine by steeping the fresh young needles in boiling water for three to five minutes. This is a fragrant and refreshing green tea, which is very high in vitamins A and C.

For those who are persistent by nature, white pine cones

have very small seeds that may be gathered from August through fall, roasted and eaten. Unlike western pines, our eastern pines have such small seeds that from our experience it isn't worth the effort except as a nibble.

The inner bark of white pine may be candied or eaten raw in emergencies. Other pine barks could be used but white pine is the sweetest. White pines are easily identified by their needles, which are three to five inches long and arranged in bundles of five. These needles are bluish green and very flexible. The cones are spindle-shaped and often curve at the end. White pines grow to be very large; it takes them up to two hundred years to reach maturity. The pliable inner bark may be gathered any time but it will be easier to peel away from the tree in the spring. Only a small patch of bark should be taken from each tree since the removal of bark will make the tree vulnerable to invasion by insects and disease. You shouldn't need much of the inner bark since a little of this candy goes a long way. To candy the bark, boil the inner strips in a mixture of two cups water to one cup of honey until pliable; cool and use as a chewing gum-type candy. This gum has a lively pine taste that takes some getting used to. The cooking liquid makes a nice honey and pine-flavored drink when sipped hot or chilled.

Other conifers whose needles may be used for teas are eastern hemlock (*Tsuga canadensis*) and northern white cedar or arborvitae (*Thuja occidentalis*). The berries of the eastern red cedar or juniper (*Juniperus virginiana*) are steeped to make a gin-flavored tea. We know people who drink this tea and claim they like it, but we have never shared their enthusiasm.

Cattails

Cattails (*Typha latifolia*; *T. angustifolia*) offer such a wide variety of foods in all seasons that they are one of our favorite wild edible plants. Cattails grow in thick patches in swampy areas around ponds, marshes, and gravel pits and are often seen in ditches along roadsides. The cattail is most frequent in the Lake Area but can be found throughout the state. The tall yellow green leaves are flat, bladelike, and usually taller than the flower spikes, which consist of one cylinder of yellowish pollen (male) above a cylinder of compact brownish down (female). After receiving the powdery pollen from the male spike, the lower, female spike fills out in approximately six weeks to form the familiar cattail that gives the plant its name.

Young cattail plants less than a foot and a half high yield shoots that are a delicately flavored vegetable raw or cooked. Hold the plant at its base and pull it from the ground. The plant should break at just the right point. Peel the shoots so that only the solid ivory part remains. The shoots may be eaten raw and they add a nice crunch, like celery, to salads. We like them sautéed in butter just until tender. The young shoots can be found as late as July and are often surrounded by cattails already producing pollen.

The green flower spikes may be gathered for eating just before they mature. Cut off both spikes when they are still contained within a sheath or when the sheath is just coming off. The cooked spikes taste like corn on the cob and are fixed in much the same way. Drop them into boiling water and cook for about 5 minutes or until the outer part is tender. Butter and salt them and eat both spikes down to the "cob." The upper male spikes are best because they are covered with a fairly thick layer of budding blossoms. Words can tell you that these spikes taste like corn, but only your taste buds will tell you that it is true. These should be a delight to corn-loving Hoosiers.

In June and July the pollen from the male flower spike matures, turning bright yellow, and the smallest nudge will send billows of yellow pollen into the air. Gather pollen by holding a plastic bag over the bent spikes and shaking them. Check the contents for any stray bugs that might try to hitch a ride home with you. The pollen can then be mixed with flour and is a delicious and colorful addition to any recipe. Eating pollen pancakes is an exceptionally nice way to begin a long day's hike. Our favorite recipe is Pollen Pancakes à la Kephart. Combine 1 cup unbleached white or whole wheat flour, 1 teaspoon baking powder, 1 teaspoon baking soda, and ¼ teaspoon salt. In another bowl combine 1 tablespoon melted butter, 1 beaten egg, and 1½ cups sour milk. (Make sour milk by adding a tablespoon of vinegar or lemon juice to the milk and allowing it to curdle for 5 minutes.) Combine 1 cup pollen with the liquid and dry ingredients. Mix quickly just to moisten. Cook ¼ cup at a time on a hot oiled griddle.

Cattail pollen may also be added to biscuits, breads, and cookies; pollen cornbread, our version of mellow yellow, is especially colorful. Replace one-half the wheat flour in your favorite cornbread recipe with pollen and enjoy. If you

gather more pollen than you can use immediately, be sure to store it in the refrigerator in a closed container, since the pollen will mold at room temperature.

Cattail roots may be gathered at any time of the year but are best in early spring or in the fall (the frost seems to make them more tender). The roots are usually larger and easier to pull if the plant is standing in water. The rootstalks just below the ground surface can be peeled and eaten raw or, since the core is almost pure starch, prepared like potatoes. The thick horizontal roots coming off the main rootstalk can be pared down to the inner portion and eaten, but they are tough and fibrous even after cooking. However, new sprouts coming from these horizontal roots are very tender and tasty if peeled and then steamed or sautéed for 5–10 minutes until tender.

Since cattails in the same patch develop at different times during the growing season, it is possible to feast on shoots, spikes, pollen, sprouts, and roots all at the same time from the same cattail patch.

When the cattails are old and soft down has begun to burst from the stalk, you can gather the down to stuff pillows, just as the Indians and pioneers did. We like the pillows so much that it has become a fall ritual to gather down for them. They make wonderful gifts to give to special friends. Make sure the down is well dried before using it for stuffing. The Miami and Potawatomie Indians padded cradles and dressed wounds with cattail down, and used the sturdy leaves to roof the rounded tops of their wigwams. The pioneers used the leaves for caulking barrels and making rush-bottomed furniture.

The cattail is truly a plant for all seasons and its uses are only limited by your imagination.

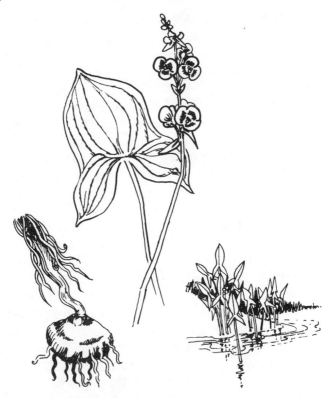

Arrowheads

Arrowheads are found on the muddy borders of streams, ponds, lakes, and ditches. The two largest species are common arrowhead (*Sagittaria latifolia*) and *Sagittaria cuneata*. Both are restricted to the Lake Area, as is stiff arrowhead (*S. rigida*). Shortbeak arrowhead (*S. brevirostra*) is found throughout the state and is the most common. Arrowheads are easily recognized by their radiant green, arrow-shaped leaves, although a few species will occasionally bear leaves that are without the characteristic wings. In summer white, three-petaled flowers are borne in whorls of three on erect flower stalks.

The roots should be gathered in late autumn, when nothing will be left standing but the brown leafstalks, so locate your colony when it is flowering or still green. Although the entire rootstalk is edible, the small white starchy tubers at the end of the long rootstalk are best. Because the tubers lie in mud several feet from the plant, Indian squaws gathered the tubers by wading barefoot in the icy water and grasping the rootstalk between their toes until the tubers were released. However, you will probably want to wear high rubber boots and use a shovel or rake to loosen the tubers from their muddy bed. A canoe or boat greatly simplifies foraging for this wild food.

The tubers are bitter when raw but when boiled or roasted become sweet like a potato. In fact the plant is often called duck potato. At one time the Indians ate a lot of arrowhead tubers and today the Chinese in the lower Sacramento Valley gather the western species of arrowhead, calling it tule potato. A species of *Sagittaria* is cultivated in China for its tuberous roots. Occasionally large cities have arrowhead tubers for sale in their Chinese markets.

We have found large colonies of arrowhead growing on the borders of Lake Monroe as well as in the Lake Area. We steam the unpeeled tubers for 30 minutes or until tender, then peel and slice them into small chunks. Sauté the sliced tubers and 1 chopped onion in butter until the onions are soft and the tubers are heated through. Salt and pepper to taste and serve topped with toasted sesame seeds. Any potato recipe may be used to prepare the tubers.

The arrowhead and the arrow arum (*Peltandra virginica*) are similar in that they both have arrow-shaped leaves and both grow in wet habitats. The arrow arum, although not poisonous, is highly astringent and unpleasant to taste. Make sure that the veins on the arrowhead leaf run parallel or straight up and down. The arrow arum has veins that are more horizontal (pinnate). In addition, the arrow arum grows to be much larger than the arrowhead. The plants are easiest to distinguish when they are flowering since the arrow arum flowers are densely clustered and enclosed in a narrow green spathe or hood.

Bulrush

All species of bulrushes have edible roots but the great American bulrush (*Scirpus validus*) is the best. Bulrushes are found in wet ground and on swamp, pond, and lake edges throughout the state. When a lake begins to dry up, bulrushes are usually the first species to occupy the area. Their tall, light green stems are naked and soft as they rise from the sheath formed by the long tapelike leaves. The flowers, which begin to appear in June, are suspended from short, branching stems in long spiky clusters near the top of the

naked stem. The small hard seeds are surrounded by bris-
tles.

Although bulrush roots have been used as a famine food in
various parts of the world, the young shoots and sprouts
were considered a delicacy by the Indians. The new sprouts
and young shoots can be eaten either raw or cooked; they are
like corresponding parts of the cattail and are prepared in
the same way. A gourmet salad can be made by marinating
the shoots and sprouts in a mixture of ½ cup olive oil and ½
cup wine vinegar. Add chopped green onions and chill for at
least 3 hours. Serve on a bed of lettuce and enjoy the feast.

Bulrush pollen, like cattail pollen, may be gathered in
early summer and substituted in recipes for half of the
wheat flour. Fried bread made with chufa flour and bulrush
pollen is a taste treat. Combine ½ cup chufa flour (or wheat
flour), ⅛ teaspoon salt, 1 teaspoon baking powder, and ½
cup bulrush pollen. Add enough milk to form a dough (ap-
prox. ½ cup) and shape into walnut-sized balls (about 8–10).
Drop the balls into hot oil and fry until they are golden
brown and bob to the top of the oil. While they are still hot,
roll them in cinnamon and brown sugar and eat them warm.

You will need a shovel to gather the edible rootstalks,
which should be dug in early spring or fall while they are
well filled out. Although the horizontal roots extending from
the main rootstalk are edible, they are usually too tough and
woody to bother with. The rootstalks are very starchy and
may be eaten raw but they are best either boiled or baked.
To make bulrush chips, slice the peeled rootstalk into pieces
⅛-inch thick, brush them with oil, and bake in a 425° oven
for 15 minutes or until tender. Turn the chips once during
the baking to brown both sides. Sprinkle with salt and eat
while they are hot.

Chufa

The roots of chufa (*Cyperus esculentus*) bear small, nutlike underground tubers that may be eaten raw or cooked. Chufa can be found in rich, wet soil along streams and in cultivated fields in southern Indiana and occasionally in the northern part of the state. The triangular-stemmed chufa, an Old World sedge, is one to three feet tall. Its pale green, ribbonlike leaves with prominent midribs originate from the

root. Shorter leaves arise high on the flower stalk and surround the golden brown flower clusters, which look like
upside-down umbrellas. The long horizontal roots end in
tubers one-half inch long that may be gathered in late autumn or early spring.

If the plant is growing in heavy clay soil, you will need a
shovel to dig up the tubers, which may be several feet away
from the plant. The dark, wrinkled tubers are both larger
and easier to gather when the plant is growing in sandy soil.
Pinch off the tubers, wash under running water, and boil
them 20 minutes, changing the water twice. To make chufa
stew, place 1 cup parboiled tubers in 3 cups salted water and
boil for 1 hour. Then replace any lost water with vegetable
bouillon, add 2 cups chopped, mixed vegetables (such as
broccoli, carrots, celery, and onions), and simmer 20 minutes longer.

To make "chufa nuts," it is necessary to boil the tubers 30
minutes in 2 changes of water. Let them drain for about 15
minutes, then fry in hot oil for 5–10 minutes. After 5 minutes
start testing to see if the tubers crunch when bitten into.
Sprinkle lightly with sea salt. These really taste like nuts.

A refreshing drink to accompany the nuts may be made by
soaking ½ pound of raw tubers in water for 48 hours, then
mashing them or puréeing them in a blender. Blend in 1
quart water and ⅓ cup mild honey. Strain and serve over
ice.

The tubers may also be ground into flour. To make chufa
flour, boil the nodules for 20 minutes, changing the water
twice. Place them on a cookie sheet and toast in a 250° oven
for 1 hour or until they are crisp enough to shatter easily
when pounded. Put the cooled tubers into a clean white sock
or plastic bread bag and, holding the open end closed, hit
the tubers lightly with a hammer or wooden mallet until
there are no noticeable lumps. The resulting flour will be
coarse. It can be used as it is or whirred in a blender to give

it a finer texture. Either way, the flour may be used in any recipe by substituting it for part of the wheat flour. We make chufa loaf by combining ½ cup chufa flour, ½ cup wheat flour, 2 teaspoons baking powder, and ½ teaspoon salt. Add 1 beaten egg, 1 teaspoon honey, and enough water to form a thick dough. Spoon the dough into a greased loaf pan and bake in a preheated 400° oven for 20 minutes. This loaf is better if eaten while it is still hot. The flavor is somewhat like coconut.

Wild Rice

Wild rice (*Zizania aquatica*), which is not a true rice, is a tall stately grass with coarse, bladelike, alternate leaves and long, broomlike, golden flower clusters. The leaves are yellow green in late spring and early summer but they become straw yellow by harvest time. The slender grain is cylindrical, black, and nearly three-fourths of an inch long. Like the cattail, wild rice is found on the mucky or boggy borders of streams and lakes and in dredged ditches, sloughs, and swamps. A native of the Great Lakes, wild rice once abounded in the many swamplands of northern Indiana, and was a favorite food of the Potawatomie Indians because it could be kept for use in the winter when other vegetable foods and meat were scarce or difficult to obtain. Because of extensive draining of our northern marshlands, wild rice has nearly disappeared from Indiana. According to some accounts it is already gone. We have never found wild rice, but we believe it is still out there someplace. We hope you are able to find this once abundant grass.

Wild rice, should you be fortunate enough to find it, can be harvested in late summer or early autumn. The Indian method for gathering the rice is probably still the best. Hold the filled-out grain heads over your boat or canoe and beat them with a stick to release the black grain. If a sheet is placed in the bottom of the canoe or boat, it will be easier to transfer the wild rice when you are ready to take it home. At home, spread out the wild rice in a warm place to dry. Then parch the grain by baking it in a 450° oven for about 1 hour, stirring occasionally so that it will parch evenly. Remove the husks by rubbing the cooled grain between your hands or pounding it with a mallet, clean out the debris, and store the rice in a tightly closed container. Be sure to rinse the rice well before cooking or it will have an unpleasant, smoky flavor.

Wild rice can be cooked in the same manner as brown rice. Rinse the rice well. Use 4 cups of water for every cup of wild rice. Bring the water to a boil, add the rice, cover and simmer on low for 50–60 minutes. Another excellent way to prepare the rice is to sauté 1 chopped onion and 1 cup sliced mushrooms in 3 tablespoons of vegetable oil until soft, then add ¾ cup rinsed wild rice, and stir to coat the grains with oil. Add 2½ cups of water and bring to a boil. Cover and reduce the heat; continue cooking for 1 hour or until the rice

is tender and fully open and all the water has been absorbed.
This makes about 3 cups.

Wild rice may also be ground into a flour that can be substituted for one-fourth to one-half the wheat flour in any
bread recipe. To make wild rice muffins, combine 1½ cups
wheat flour, ½ cup wild rice flour, 2 teaspoons baking powder, and ¼ teaspoon salt. In another bowl combine 2 tablespoons honey, 1 beaten egg, 1 cup milk, and ¼ cup oil. Mix
together the liquid and dry ingredients, stirring just enough
to moisten. Fill greased muffin tins two-thirds full and bake
in a preheated 400° oven for 20 minutes. These muffins are
best eaten warm with thick pats of melting butter.

In Indiana the grasses make up one-tenth of our entire
flora and many of them have edible seeds. Crab grass, that
common foe of manicured lawns, yields seeds that are flavorful when parched and ground and eaten as cereal. Barnyard
grass (*Echinochloa crusgalli*), goose grass (*Eleusine indica*),
green foxtail grass (*Setaria viribis*), manna grass (*Glyceria
septentrionalis*), and southern cane (*Arundinaria gigantea*)
are only a few of the grasses that yield very small edible
seeds. Unfortunately, a day of collecting seldom garners
more than a cupful. If you do persevere and manage to gather
enough to bother with, boil them in water just barely to
cover until they are mush. Add this to bread dough or eat it
as a cereal.

Skunk Cabbage

Skunk cabbage (*Symplocarpus foetidus*), like all members of the Arum Family, is edible only if certain precautions are taken first. Skunk cabbage grows in colonies in shady, swampy places scattered throughout the northern two-thirds of the state. It is one of the first plants to bloom in the spring. Before its leaves appear, it pushes up a purplish brown or green mottled hood that encloses a round fleshy spike covered with small lavender flowers. In keeping with its name, skunk cabbage has an unpleasant odor.

Skunk cabbage leaves should be gathered for eating when they are still tightly furled and look like small green cigars. Boil them in at least 3 changes of water, replacing darkened water with boiling water until the water stays clear. The cooked greens usually taste peppery and can be used to make skunk cabbage lasagna, which is delicious despite its name. Cook 6 spinach lasagna noodles. Meanwhile sauté ½ pound sliced mushrooms, 2 minced garlic cloves, and 1 large chopped onion in 2 tablespoons of oil until soft. Add the drained, chopped tomatoes from a 1-pound can, 2 cups tomato purée, and 1 teaspoon each oregano, basil, and salt. Simmer 10 minutes, uncovered. Combine 2 cups creamed cottage cheese, 2 beaten eggs, 3 tablespoons grated Parmesan cheese, and 1 cup cooked skunk cabbage. In a large casserole dish put ⅓ of the tomato sauce, then ½ of the cheese mixture, then 3 cooked noodles. Repeat the layers and top with the remaining sauce. Sprinkle with 2 tablespoons grated Parmesan, cover, and bake at 350°. After 30 minutes uncover and sprinkle with ½ cup grated Mozzarella; bake uncovered 15 minutes longer. Let the lasagna cool for 10 minutes before cutting it.

The roots can be gathered in late autumn and early spring when they are well filled out. They are hard to dig and, once dug, must be dried for at least five weeks or boiled for three days. The Indians left the roots in pits with hot coals for two to three days before eating them. This sounds like the best method, but we have never tried the roots. Calcium oxalate, which is found throughout the plant, causes a choking sensation in the mouth and throat if the roots have not been roasted long enough to destroy it. All members of the Arum Family, including jack-in-the-pulpit, calamus, and arrow arum (all of which are found in Indiana), contain calcium oxalate. The roots of these plants are rendered edible only by careful preparation and are extremely fiery if underprepared. Since these arum plants yield such lovely wildflowers, we have chosen to admire them rather than eat them.

Day Lily

The day lily (*Hemerocallis fulva*), a native of Eurasia, escaped from pioneer gardens to invade roadsides and the borders of fields and woods until it has become a true weed. The bright orange flowers are still a favorite ornamental and, either wild or domestic, can be seen throughout the state. The plant propagates entirely by its many tuberous roots and is so prolific that once established, it takes over, crowding out other plants to form a pure stand of day lilies. The narrow, tapering, light green leaves originate from the rootstalk crowns. Each tall flower stalk bears eight or nine orange blossoms, which open one or two at a time. From June through August the flowers may be gathered and eaten. You needn't feel remorse for picking the succulent blossoms since each flower lasts only one day and the plant produces a succession of them.

The unopened flower buds may be added to soup or dropped into salted boiling water to cook 4 minutes. They will turn bright green and should be crunchy like fresh cooked green beans. Drain the buds and dress them while still hot with a mixture of ½ cup sour cream and 1 teaspoon lemon

juice. Both the buds and the opened flowers may be sun-dried between screens and put into tightly covered jars for later use. To reconstitute the dried buds and flowers, soak them in water for 5–10 minutes, then add to vegetable soup or stew.

The flowers can be made into flower fritters. Make a batter by combining 1 cup unbleached white or whole wheat flour, 1 teaspoon baking powder, and a dash of salt; add 1 well-beaten egg and ½ cup milk. The batter should be just thick enough to coat the flowers. If it is too thin, add more flour; if too thick, more milk. Dip the flowers in the batter and deep fry them in hot oil (360°) until golden brown. After draining on paper towels, transfer the fritters to a serving platter and drizzle with honey. Serve them hot. We fixed day lily flowers for a friend of ours visiting from California and he declared the fritters food fit for kings.

Day lily bulbs may be boiled or baked like potatoes. Serve with butter, sour cream, or cheese sauce. There are reports of day lily bulbs being toxic to some people, so eat sparingly until you are sure of your tolerance.

The young shoots make good eating if they are boiled quickly in water and drained thoroughly before serving. The shoots should not be boiled for more than 4 or 5 minutes or they will become slippery. Be sure to drain well in a colander—they tend to retain water. Serve them with butter, sour cream, or cheese sauce.

Another flower often seen blooming alongside the day lily is the yucca or Spanish bayonet (*Yucca filamentosa*). Its long, stiff, sharp-pointed leaves, which have loose threads curling from their edges, form a rosette around the tall, woody flower stalk from which hang bell-like, creamy white flow-ers. These flowers are a beautiful and palatable addition to salads.

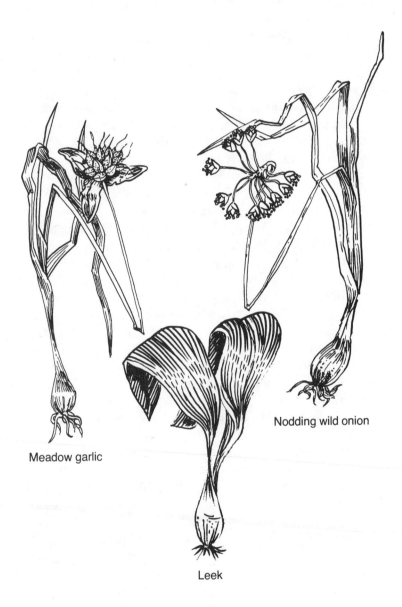

Meadow garlic

Nodding wild onion

Leek

Wild Onion, Garlic, and Leek

These three plants, the most common and most easily found of the wild edible foods, belong to the Allium Tribe. Often, as you walk across a wet meadow or beside a stream, these plants announce themselves by the characteristic onion aroma that fills the air. From April to June the wild leek (*Allium tricoccum*) can be found scattered throughout Indiana. It prefers slopes and woods near streams, and it is most often associated with beech and maple woods. The broad, one- to three-inch-wide leaves wither before the umbels of greenish white to pink flowers appear at the top of a naked stalk. Both the elongated bulb at the base and the leaves have a very strong onion smell.

One May day we found wild leeks growing so abundantly in Lawrence County that we gathered great bunches of them from the many scattered patches. We dug up the bulbs with a garden trowel, washed them in a fast-moving stream, and made plans to fix them in soup, omelets, and casseroles. Not content to wait, we prepared some immediately by chopping up a large bunch and frying them along with sliced potatoes in hot oil. Just before serving we topped them with shredded colby cheese. A wild meal cooked over a campfire in nature's kitchen adds a whole new dimension to eating.

The leaves of nodding wild onion (*Allium cernuum*) are usually more slender than those of wild leeks but very similar in appearance. The flowers range from white to deep pink. Wild onion bulbs are usually three to ten inches below the ground and, like leeks, are oblong. Nodding wild onion has a wide distribution and range of habitat, varying from high, dry banks of streams to low sedge marshes, springy places, and gravelly bars in rivers. The bulbs may be dug up from May to August and can be used like cultivated onions although their taste may be a little stronger. They were an important source of food for the Indians, who usually stored a great many for winter use. We cook wild onion bulbs in a broth with cornmeal dumplings as the Indians did. Drop 10–14 cleaned bulbs into gently boiling, seasoned broth along with 2 unpeeled, diced potatoes and 2 diced carrots. Mix up the dumplings by blending 1 cup cornmeal, 2 tablespoons butter, and ½ teaspoon salt with a pastry blender. Add 1 beaten egg and enough milk or water to moisten. Drop by spoonfuls into the bubbling broth and cook over medium heat for 20 minutes. Just before serving add some of the fresh green onion leaves chopped like chives. This is a very colorful and delicious soup. The chopped leaves are also a nice addition to salads, omelets, or whatever you want to add a little zest to.

Meadow garlic (*Allium canadense*) is prolific throughout the state from May to July in rich woods, moist thickets, hillsides, and cultivated fields. It is so abundant in the southwestern counties that it is considered a pernicious weed by farmers whose cows eat the garlic and give garlic-flavored milk. The bulbs, easy to identify by their odor and the characteristic cloves, are about a third of an inch thick and are usually found in clusters two inches underground. (The flower stalk too bears tiny edible bulblets.) We take several bulbs, peel the cloves, and put them in a jar with vegetable oil. In a few hours, we have garlic oil that can be used in salad dressings and for frying. It can also be added to bread dough to make a nice garlic-flavored bread. The oil can be replenished as it is used, for the wild garlic is strong enough to flavor several additions of oil. Our friend, Charlotte Gulling, makes garlic soup at the first hint of a cold. However, this soup is so delicious you don't need to wait until you are sick to enjoy it. To make Charlotte's Garlic Soup, peel and chop 25 garlic cloves. Sauté them in ¼ cup olive oil until they just begin to turn golden. Add 8 cups vegetable stock, 2 tablespoons tamari sauce, ¼ teaspoon each of sage and black pepper, ½ teaspoon each of oregano, thyme, and paprika, and 8 parsley sprigs. Cover and bring to a boil, then simmer for one hour. Adjust seasonings and just before serving add ½ cup dry sherry if desired. Ladle the soup into ovenproof bowls, top with toast (sourdough French bread is best), sprinkle with a mixture of Gruyère and Parmesan cheese, and broil to melt cheese. This makes 8 one-cup servings.

All members of the Allium Tribe are best identified by their odor. Do not eat bulbs that do not have a distinctive onion odor. Also, when gathering these plants, as with all plants, remember to dig up only a few bulbs from each of the scattered patches so that you won't make a noticeable impact on any one patch.

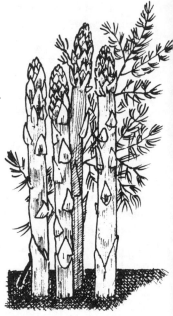

Wild Asparagus

In early spring the wild asparagus tips begin pushing their way through the soil. The spears rise from the ground as simple stems and are identical to cultivated asparagus and taste as good or better. Wild asparagus (*Asparagus officinalis*) is a garden escape that has become a common sight along fencerows and roadsides scattered throughout the state. The best way to find the tender shoots hidden among all the spring growth is to stake your claim the preceding summer. At this time the asparagus is several feet high, branched, and has light green, fernlike foliage. Later, many small red berries appear, giving the plant the look of a Christmas tree. In late fall, the foliage turns a lovely butterscotch yellow and is very conspicuous along roadsides and fencerows. Note the location of this bushy plant and wait until next April or May.

In late summer the seeds may be gathered, dried, and roasted to use as a coffee substitute. The seeds are used in Europe for this purpose. We cannot recommend the drink but we can recommend the spears. We know a special meandering country road in Pulaski County that follows the Tippecanoe River and yields several good-sized stands of asparagus. We prefer eating the vegetables steamed with butter or topped with cheese sauce. Wild asparagus can be used in any recipe calling for cultivated asparagus. Charlotte's Asparagus Soup is a great compliment to this delicately flavored vegetable. To prepare, wash about 1 pound of asparagus, cut off the tips, and keep them separate. Cut the rest in pieces about 1 inch long and boil in a pint of water for about 30 minutes. Strain and use the liquid for stock. Discard the boiled stalks; all the flavor has boiled out of them. Simmer the asparagus tips in the asparagus stock until just tender (5 to 10 minutes), then strain, reserving the stock, and set tips aside. Melt ¼ cup butter in a saucepan, add ¼ cup of wheat flour, and cook for about 2 minutes over low heat, stirring frequently. Mix the asparagus stock with 2 cups milk and add a little at a time to the flour and butter mixture, stirring until all the liquid is absorbed. Simmer and stir for another 5 minutes until slightly thickened. Add the asparagus tips, salt and nutmeg to taste, and ½ to 1 cup of yogurt or sour cream. Heat gently once more (do not boil) and serve the soup with chopped parsley sprinkled on top. This makes 4 servings.

In the fall after the first frost, the mature, bushy plant that has turned bright yellow makes a handsome decoration inside the home.

To the forager, the asparagus is truly the aristocrat of wild gardens.

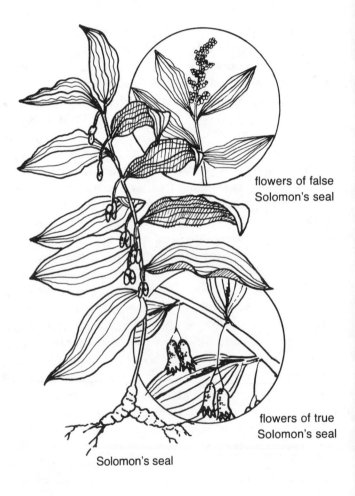

flowers of false
Solomon's seal

flowers of true
Solomon's seal

Solomon's seal

Solomon's Seal and False Solomon's Seal

Solomon's seal (*Polygonatum biflorum*) is a large plant of the Lily Family with pointed, oval, many-ribbed leaves that are light green above and pale beneath. The alternate, stalkless leaves are arranged on a round, stout stem. In April through June, paired yellow green flowers appear; these dangle from the leaf axils and are hidden beneath the gracefully arching plant. The flowers are followed by green berries that turn blue black as they ripen. Solomon's seal can be found in a wide variety of habitats throughout the state—in moist woodlands, in open places, and along roadsides and fences.

The large, tender shoots, which consist of a single shaft with tightly wrapped leaves, can be eaten as a green vegetable and are like asparagus. To prepare the shoots, peel off the outer skin with a sharp knife. Be careful not to cut into the shoots too deeply or they will break. Lay them in a large skillet; add 2 cups of water and ¼ teaspoon salt. Bring to a boil over medium heat, reduce the heat, and allow to boil gently for 15 minutes or until the shoots are tender but still firm. Serve immediately with butter or cheese. These cooked shoots may also be chilled and served with a mixture of 6 tablespoons olive oil, 2 tablespoons lemon juice, ½ teaspoon salt, and freshly ground pepper. The shoots are also good raw with a little salad dressing. The thick, edible roots, which have large circular scars or "seals," were used by the Indians to make flour for bread. The roots are cubed, then dried, and ground into a flour that can be substituted for part of the wheat flour in bread recipes. The roots are buried deep in the ground and require a little digging.

Another member of the Lily Family closely resembling true Solomon's seal is false Solomon's seal (*Smilacina racemosa*). This plant is scattered throughout the state in beech and sugar maple woods and black and white oak woods. It prefers shaded streamsides. The tapering oval leaves are blue green and nearly stalkless. The flowers, large terminal clusters of greenish white flowers, bloom in May through July. The berries are green at first and later turn red, making the plant very conspicuous when other plants are losing their foliage. The red berries were called scurvy berries by the pioneers and are indeed rich in vitamin C. The Indians also ate large quantities of them. However, we find that these slightly bitter berries are highly laxative when eaten in abundance.

The Indians also ate the large, fragrant roots but to rid them of their bitter taste they were first soaked in ashes that had been mixed with water and then boiled for a short while to eliminate the ash "lye." Like true Solomon's seal, the young shoots make a good asparaguslike vegetable.

Greenbriar

It is nice to know that this troublesome plant has some usefulness. There are several species of greenbriar in Indiana; all have edible shoots. The young shoots and growing tip-ends of greenbriar are good raw or cooked and the young, barely unrolling leaves make an excellent nibble. One of the most commonly eaten varieties is roundleaf greenbriar (*Smilax rotundifolia*), which has heart-shaped, pointed leaves about two inches across and three inches long. It is found primarily in the southern counties, as is sawbriar (*S. glauca* var. *genuina*). Fringe greenbriar (*S. bona-nox*) is found only in the high hills near the Ohio River. For the most part, greenbriar is common in the southern counties, rare in the northern part of the state, and seldom seen in central Indiana. Most greenbriars prefer dry soil in woods, clearings, and abandoned fields and if left undisturbed form impenetrable thickets. The long thorny vines bear clusters of blue black unpalatable berries about a quarter-inch in diameter. In May through August the tender green new shoots and new tips of older vines are gathered by breaking them off only as far down on the vine as will snap easily between the fingers. They must be young or they will be woody. In places where greenbriar is found there is usually a lot of it scattered through the woods. For this reason, a good way to gather the new tip-end growth is to keep an eye out as you are walking through the woods. Gathering it casually as you are hiking takes a lot of the tedium out of getting enough of the delicate tip-ends to make a worthwhile serving.

The shoots give a crisp texture to salads or they may be steamed in serving-size bundles like asparagus. We like them served hot with cheese sauce or chilled and mixed with mayonnaise and hard-boiled eggs. This yellow green plant is rich in vitamins A and C.

Greenbriar has whitish, cordlike roots that turn red when exposed to the air. They contain a principle like pectin that makes it very easy to make jelly from them. The roots should be dug in the early spring or in the autumn when they are well filled out. Chop or grind the roots, then cover with water, and boil for an hour until the water is very dark. Strain and combine the liquid with half as much honey as you have liquid. Boil for about 15 minutes, then pour into jars, and allow it to cool. After it cools, you will have a soft rustcolored jelly. Store in the refrigerator and use as a jelly or dilute with water for a sweet drink.

Carrion-flower (*S. herbacea*) looks like greenbriar but it is not so woody and does not have prickles. Although infrequent in the state, it is most often found in beech and white oak woods. Like greenbriar, the young shoots and growing tip-ends are edible.

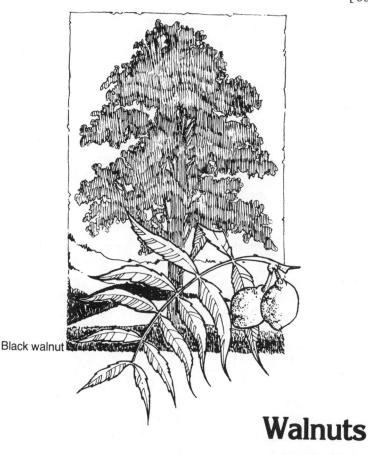

Black walnut

Walnuts

Indiana lies in the heart of the walnut belt and the black walnut (*Juglans nigra*) is common throughout the state. Although once common in dense woods, it is now most often seen along fences, roadsides, and the borders of woods. Its large, alternate compound leaves, one to two feet long, contain seven to twenty-three leaflets. Quite often there is no end leaflet. The leaflets, three to four inches long, are sharply pointed and toothed along the margins. The rough, dark-brown bark has prominent ridges and deep furrows.

The thick-shelled, oily nuts are nearly round and enclosed in a yellowish green hull that later turns brown-black. Walnuts are high in protein, having 50% more protein pound for pound than meat.

In September and October the nuts may be gathered and eaten fresh or roasted. After you have gathered the nuts, they must be hulled and dried. The hulls are hard to remove but one way to get them off is to run over them with a car. Be sure to wear gloves when handling the freshly hulled nuts as the brown stain is impossible to wash off. After they are hulled, spread them out and let them dry for two or three weeks. Then they are ready to be cracked and the nutmeats picked out. As far as we know, there is no easy method for extracting the delicious nutmeats. A hammer, a nutpick, and a willingness for labor are needed to release the sweet nutmeats from their shells.

Walnut meal is a nutritious addition to breads or cookies. To grind, simply put the shelled nuts in a blender until the nuts are reduced to a meal. We like to make black walnut loaf with this meal. To prepare the loaf, chop and steam a large bunch of wild greens (lamb's quarters, purslane, dock, or sorrel) for 5 minutes. Then sauté ½ cup chopped wild onions, 2 tablespoons chopped parsley, 1 mashed wild garlic clove, and 1 teaspoon oregano in ¼ cup of oil. Combine the sautéed seasonings and the steamed greens with 2 cups black walnut meal, 1 cup whole wheat bread crumbs, ½ cup sesame seeds, ½ cup tomato sauce, and 1 tablespoon tamari sauce. Shape into a loaf and bake in a preheated 350° oven for 30 minutes. Served with additional tomato sauce, this hearty main dish resembles meat loaf.

The Indians boiled the walnut kernels in water and skimmed off the oil to use as a sweet-flavored cooking oil. Both Indians and pioneers used the husks around the shells along with the bark to produce a brown dye. The walnut tree has high commercial value and is an excellent tree to plant as a future investment. But take care not to plant walnut trees very near a garden since the tree produces a toxin with an inhibiting effect on the growth of tomatoes, potatoes, and other plants. The tree grows rapidly but is hard to transplant because of its long taproot. Many of the black walnuts seen today have been planted by humans or industrious squirrels.

The white walnut or butternut (*Juglans cinerea*) is very similar in appearance to the black walnut. The bark is gray with wide, flat, shiny ridges. The butternut, which is found infrequently throughout the state, prefers well-drained, gravelly soils along streams and in ravines but is also found in rich, moist woods and bottomlands. The Potawatomie Indians drank a tea made from the inner bark of the butternut for stomach upsets. And we have heard that concentrated butternut sap can be collected in the spring and made into a syrup like maple syrup. Butternuts are oblong and have a hairy, sticky, nonsplitting husk. This sweet, oily nut can be used in the same manner as the black walnut.

Green immature butternuts may be gathered in early summer and pickled, husk and all. Use nuts that are soft enough to be pierced with a nut pick. First add the nuts to boiling water and boil until the water becomes dark. Pour off the dark water, add freshly boiling water, and continue cooking until the nuts are barely tender. Now pack the nuts into hot, sterilized quart canning jars. To each jar add 1 teaspoon pickling spices, then cover the nuts with a mixture of hot vinegar and honey. The proportion of vinegar and honey can vary according to individual taste; we use a one-to-one ratio. Seal and process 15 minutes in a boiling water bath. The pickles are ready to eat in 6–8 weeks.

Butternut wood is soft, so the tree does not have the commercial value of black walnut. However, the quality of the nuts alone, not to mention the beauty of the tree, should encourage anyone to plant the butternut.

Shagbark hickory

Hickories

The shagbark hickory (*Carya ovata*) is the best known of all hickories. It is a large, stately tree that often reaches a height of one hundred feet with a trunk diameter of three feet or more. The shagbark is found in every county of the state, usually in moist, rich woodlands. It has compound alternate leaves eight to fourteen inches long, each with five leaflets. The two leaflets nearest the base are usually half the size of the three upper ones. The bark is gray and on older trees distinctively shaggy, splitting into thin strips that separate from the trunk at either end but cling tightly in the center. The nuts, one- to one-and-a-half inches long, are enclosed in hulls that split easily into four parts to expose the hard shells. The large white kernel inside is very sweet. Hickory nuts are justly popular and every year a great many are gathered and sold in the markets. The Indians gathered them by the bushel and made shagbark syrup by pounding the kernels and shells in a mortar for a very long time, until the nuts were rendered a fine powder. Then they added water and pounded the nut meal until a milky or oily syrup was produced.

The thickness of the shells and the sweetness of the nutmeats will vary from tree to tree, so look for a tree with thin-shelled, flavorful nuts. A good method of cracking the nuts is to hit them squarely on their broad side with a hammer. In most instances the nuts will open perfectly, releasing whole kernels; however, we have found some nuts with such thick, hard shells that we suspected that nothing short of dynamite could ever open them. The nutmeats will come out more easily if the nuts are roasted in a slow oven or allowed to air dry. If you do not want to roast the nuts, just spread them out in a warm, sunny place that is protected from animal bandits for about three weeks. Then crack and use in any recipe calling for nuts.

Nuts are high in protein and make an excellent main dish when made into creamy nut soup. Take shelled hickory nuts (or pecans) and grind in the blender until you have 1 cup of fine nut meal. Cook the ground nuts in 3 cups milk over low heat for 15 minutes while stirring constantly. Remove from heat. Add a little of the warm nut milk to 2 beaten egg yolks, then add the yolk-milk mixture to the nut milk in the pan. Add ¼ cup apple juice and 1 teaspoon honey. Simmer 5 minutes but do not boil or it will curdle. Blend in the blender and serve garnished with additional chopped hickory nuts (or pecans) and slivered apples.

The bigleaf shellbark (*C. laciniosa*) is very similar to the shagbark hickory in size and appearance but in general is not as shaggy. A distinguishing characteristic is that the compound leaves usually contain seven leaflets, although occasionally there are five or nine. The bigleaf shellbark is scattered throughout the state, but it is most frequent in the Lower Wabash Valley and nearly absent in the north-western counties. The mockernut or white hickory (*C. to-mentosa*) is usually found associated with the bigleaf shellbark in the Lower Wabash Valley. Both trees bear sweet, edible nuts. The small-fruited hickory (*C. ovalis*) bears small, thin-shelled nuts with fairly sweet kernels. The compound leaves usually have seven leaflets. This tree bears nuts more often than any other hickory and is found primarily north of the Wabash River. The pignut hickory (*C. glabra*) is found throughout the state, especially in the southern part. The husks of its nuts are pear-shaped. We find that the nuts of this tree are often bitter and unpalatable. As long as they are sweet, the nuts of all hickories are edible and may be used interchangeably although they will vary in size and quality. There are reports that hickories may be tapped in the spring for their sap just as maples are, but we have never tried this.

The pecan (*C. illinoensis*), another member of the Hickory Family, is found in the southwestern part of the state, primarily in river bottomlands following the Wabash River as far north as Covington in Fountain County and eastward along the Ohio River to Clark County. It is also found up the White River into Greene County and up the Muscatatuck River into Washington County. We have found a great many pecan trees growing along fencerows in Posey County. The pecan has a tight-fitting bark that rarely becomes scaly but is moderately rough with furrows and brown ridges. The alternate compound leaves usually bear thirteen leaflets although occasionally there are as few as nine or as many as seventeen. The leaflets are usually slightly curved or sickle-shaped. The elongated small nut with its sweet kernel is considered one of the best nuts of any native American tree. Indians valued the pecan so much that they believed that the Great Spirit himself was present in the pecan tree. Paccan, the Miami Indian chief who succeeded Little Turtle in 1812, was named in honor of the pecan. *Paccan* is the Algonquin word that *pecan* is derived from.

Unfortunately, only one out of every four wild pecan trees in Indiana bears nuts. If you manage to find enough, these sweet nuts are good in breads, cookies, cakes, pies, or just about anything you can dream up. An excellent nut bread can be made by combining 2½ cups whole wheat flour, 2½ teaspoons baking powder, ½ teaspoon baking soda, and ½ teaspoon of salt. In another bowl, cream 2 tablespoons of butter with 1 cup of honey, then add 1 beaten egg and 1½ tablespoons of grated orange rind and mix. Add the creamed mixture to the dry ingredients alternately with ¾ cup orange juice. Fold in ¾ cup chopped pecans. Bake in a greased loaf pan in a 325° oven for 60–70 minutes. This bread will slice better and have a moister texture if allowed to stand a day before it is eaten. Other juices or strong infusions of herbal teas may be substituted for the orange juice if you prefer. If you use herbal teas, substitute grated lemon rind for the orange rind.

American Hazelnut

The American hazelnut (*Corylus americana*) is a shrub found scattered throughout the state in rich woods and open thickets and along the borders of woods, fences, and roadsides. Although the hazelnut adapts well to either moist or dry soil, it does best in the black loam soils of northern Indiana. We have gathered large quantities of hazelnuts along abandoned railroad tracks in Fulton County. The hazelnut is a many-branched shrub that grows in large spreading clumps. Its alternate simple leaves, two to five inches long, are egg-shaped and sharply double-toothed, with the teeth pointing toward the tip of the leaf. The hazelnut flowers in March or early April and the nuts ripen in late July to October. The thick hard nuts are partly enclosed in a downy casing and resemble commercial filberts. These nuts are easily collected and remain on the shrub through autumn, but you will have to hurry if you hope to beat chipmunks and other small creatures to them. Since chipmunks cannot climb tall trees, this shrub is just right for them.

Crunchy hazelnut cakes like those the Indians ate can be made by grinding ½ pound of shelled hazelnuts in a blender or nut grinder and boiling the meal in 2 cups of water, stirring occasionally, until the mixture resembles mush. Add ⅓ cup cornmeal and 1 teaspoon salt and let stand for 20 minutes until thickened. Heat ½ cup oil in a large 12-inch skillet until a drop of water flicked on it sizzles. Drop the dough by tablespoonfuls into the hot oil. Brown well on one side, turn, flatten the cake with a well-greased spatula, and brown. Serve hot or cold as bread.

The taste of hazelnuts is reminiscent of coconut, and honey nut custard ice cream is an excellent combination of flavors. To prepare, pour 1⅔ cups evaporated milk into freezing trays and freeze until ice crystals form around edges of the tray. In a pan combine ⅛ teaspoon salt with 4 well-beaten egg yolks and add 2 cups boiling water very slowly. Be sure to stir constantly. Cook over hot water or in a double boiler for 2 minutes. Cool and add 1 cup honey. Whip the chilled evaporated milk until it is stiff. Fold the honey mixture into the whipped milk and add ½ cup chopped hazelnuts. Pour back into the freezing trays and freeze until firm. Scoop out and serve topped with warmed honey and more chopped hazelnuts.

The hazelnut shrub makes an excellent screen hedge around homes since it reaches a height of six or seven feet. Hazelnuts are also recommended along fences and near woodlands, where they will serve as a low windbreak, provide shelter for birds, and supply food for game. The hazelnut is easily propagated by planting the nuts in fall or spring. The shrub grows rapidly, forming mats of numerous root shoots. The hazelnut is a plant worth knowing and growing.

American Chestnut

This handsome tree (*Castanea dentata*) once flourished in
the forests of America. It was plentiful in Indiana, and
chestnuts were an important food for the Indians and
pioneers. But, at the turn of the century there appeared a
fungus that attacks the trunk and branches of chestnuts,
forming cankers and eventually killing the tree. The blight
was first reported in 1904 in New York where it had inadver-
tently been introduced from Japan. It spread like an
epidemic, killing most of the chestnut trees. The chestnut
blight reached Indiana in the early 1930s. By the mid-1930s
nearly every natural stand of American chestnut in the eastern United States was dead or suffering from the blight.
Today natural stands of the American chestnut are restricted
to sandy soil and limestone outcrops in south-central Indiana. The greatest number are found in Clark, Crawford,
Floyd, Jackson, Harrison, and Washington counties. Chestnuts are associated with black, white, and scarlet oaks. Mature chestnut bark is grayish brown and deeply furrowed.
The simple alternate leaves, six to eight inches long, have
sharply pointed ends and coarsely toothed margins, and are
glossy green above and pale underneath. The late-blooming

flowers appear in June or July. The honey-colored flowers are long and slender and resemble pipe cleaners, especially as they dry up and fall off the tree. They have a strong scent that is very noticeable.

The flowers are followed by green prickly burrs, which mature in September or October. After a frost the mature burrs burst open to release one to three dark brown shiny nuts, which are delicious when boiled or roasted. If you have never eaten chestnuts, you are in for a wonderful taste experience. The nutritious kernels are seven percent fat and eleven percent protein and contain phosphorus, potassium, magnesium, and sulphur. We like chestnuts best when they

are freshly roasted. First, make a cross-shaped slit on the flat side of each chestnut, then put them into a pan with 1 teaspoon of vegetable oil. Shake the pan to coat the chestnuts with oil. Roast in a preheated 350° oven until the shells and inner skins can be easily removed. After roasting they may be eaten immediately or cooled and ground into a flour and used in breads. Substitute chestnut flour for one half of the wheat flour and prepare as usual.

Roasted chestnuts may also be made into chestnut purée. Cover the shelled, roasted nuts with water and add 1 tablespoon vinegar, 3 stalks coarsely chopped celery, and 1 small, coarsely chopped onion. Boil until tender, then drain off the excess liquid. Purée in the blender until smooth. Add 2 tablespoons melted butter, 3 tablespoons heavy cream, and salt and pepper to taste. Serve topped with a pat of butter. To make chestnut soup, just dilute the puréed chestnuts with extra cream until the desired consistency is reached.

At their nursery in Jackson County the Indiana Division of Forestry is working to develop a strain of chestnuts able to withstand the chestnut blight. We visited the nursery at Vallonia and discovered that the American chestnut has not altogether disappeared. Through careful genetic hybridization and selection an effort is being made to develop disease-resistant trees. Many disease-resistant trees are still found growing wild and a search for and citing of such trees was recently made in Dubois County. Seeds collected from the resistant trees are used for hybridization to develop a genetically blight-resistant line of the American chestnut. Steve Pennington, the resident expert on the American chestnut, told us that Richard Janes at the Connecticut Agricultural Experiment Station in New Haven has recently discovered that introducing a benign European chestnut fungus into diseased trees will drive out the fungus that causes the chestnut blight. We may yet see the revival of the American chestnut!

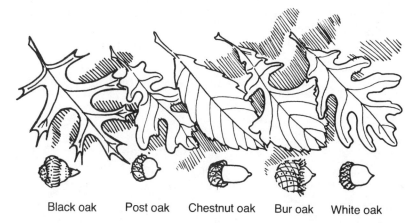

Black oak   Post oak   Chestnut oak   Bur oak   White oak

Oaks

The seventeen native oaks make up the largest group of forest trees native to Indiana. They can be divided into two major categories: white oaks and black oaks. All oaks have simple alternate leaves. Members of the white oak group have leaves with rounded lobes and, because they mature their acorns in a single year, are called annual oaks. Black oaks have bristle-tipped leaves; they take two years to mature their acorns and are sometimes called biennial oaks. All oaks produce edible acorns, but those of white oaks are sweeter. The acorns of black oaks are bitter due to their tannin content, which must be leached out before they can be eaten. White oak acorns are usually sweet and require little or no leaching. Hoosier pioneers roasted white acorns to eat with meat in place of bread, and early settlers of Wayne County used white acorns ground into flour as a grain substitute. In other parts of Indiana, to tide themselves over until the corn was harvested, pioneers made ash cakes from roasted white acorns pounded together with wild rice and wild barley. The sweetest white oaks in Indiana are the post oak (*Quercus stellata*) and the chestnut oak (*Q. prinus* and *Q. montana*). The separate species of oak may be difficult to identify precisely because they tend to hybridize and back-cross.

The post oak was given its name by the pioneers, who made fence posts from its very durable wood. Post oak is usually found in the southwestern and south-central counties. Its coarse, leathery leaves are four to six inches long and dark green and shiny on top with a heavy coating of rusty brown hairs underneath. The dark brown acorn is about one-half inch long and often it is striped. The shallow cup, which is covered with woolly scales, encloses about one-third of the nut. The bark is dark and rough and slightly scaly.

The chestnut oak has stiff leaves that are five to nine inches long with coarse, rounded teeth. The large, chestnut brown acorn, which is one- to one-and-a-half inches long, is oval and glossy smooth. On older trunks the bark is thick, brown black, and deeply furrowed with high, sharp, angular ridges. This oak also is restricted to the southwestern and south-central counties.

Although the post oak and the chestnut oaks are the sweetest, there are other white oaks scattered throughout Indiana that bear sweet edible nuts requiring a minimum amount of leaching. These include the white oak (*Q. alba*), the swamp white oak (*Q. bicolor*), the bur oak (*Q. macrocarpa*) and the chinquapin oak (*Q. muhlenbergii*). In addition, the overcup oak (*Q. lyrata*) is found in the southwestern counties.

A few of the black oaks commonly found in Indiana are the black oak (*Q. velutina*), the red oak (*Q. borealis*), and the pin oak (*Q. palustris*). We have eaten the acorns of both white and black oaks but prefer the lazy preparation of those from white oaks. Although the acorns of some white oak species may require a short leaching period, all from black oaks require long, thorough leaching.

We tried several leaching methods. The following is the simplest and can be used for the acorns of either white or black oaks. Collect ripe acorns in the fall, taking care not to choose any with worm holes. With a sharp knife slit the shells, remove them, and boil the acorns for at least 2 hours. Each time the water turns light brown, replace it with fresh, boiling water. (By removing the tannin, boiling sweetens the acorns and turns them dark brown.) When the water stays clear, the acorns are ready to roast in a preheated 350° oven for 1 hour. After roasting they can be eaten plain or ground into a nutty-tasting flour. To make the flour, chop the boiled, roasted acorns; then grind them in a flour mill, blender, or food grinder. Toast the flour in the oven for ½ hour. If a fine-textured flour is desired, put it through the grinder at least two more times.

This flour can be used to make an Indian-style bread. Combine 1 cup acorn flour, ½ cup cornmeal, ½ cup whole wheat flour, 1 teaspoon salt, and 1 teaspoon baking powder. In another bowl combine 3 tablespoons oil, ¼ cup honey, 1 egg, and 1 cup milk. Add this mixture to the dry ingredients. Bake at 350° for 20–30 minutes in a well-greased 8 x 8 x 2 inch square pan. This bread smells sweet and nutty while baking, and it is delicious eaten warm and topped with slabs of butter.

Acorn cookies can be made by blending ½ cup oil with ½ cup honey. Beat in 2 eggs and then add 1 cup coarsely ground acorn flour and 1 cup whole wheat flour. Fold in ½ cup leached, finely chopped acorns. Drop the batter by teaspoonfuls onto a lightly oiled cookie sheet. Bake in a 375° oven for 15 minutes.

Red mulberry

Mulberries

The red mulberry (*Morus rubra*) is known by nearly all Hoosiers since it is scattered throughout every county in the state. This small tree is abundantly distributed by birds and can be found in sunny places along fences and roadsides. The three- to five-inch-long leaves are simple and alternate. Like the sassafras, the mulberry has variable leaves. Besides roundish leaves with no lobes there are two- and three-lobed leaves. The three-lobed leaves resemble fleurs-de-lis. The leaves are dark green, toothed, and short-tipped with deeply sunken veins on the upper surface, which is rough to the touch. The leafstalks will give a milky secretion if squeezed. The soft, fleshy, many-seeded berries are dark red to black and three-fourths to one-and-a-half inches long. The sweet and juicy berries are sought after by people, birds, and other animals. The best way to gather the berries is by shaking heavily laden branches over an old sheet or blanket. You can gather a gallon easily and quickly in this manner. Eat them as they fall or take them home and make mulberry juice cocktails by pressing the berries through a colander to extract the juice. Add a little lemon and a touch of mild-flavored honey. Chill and serve over ice.

We should warn you that these berries leave telltale stains of purple on your hands and lips, but the taste is so good you probably won't care. The berries may be served with yogurt or baked into pies or spooned into crêpes. Cheesecake lovers should take note that chilled mulberries are a great accompaniment to that creamy dessert. Another favorite of ours is mulberry cobbler. Place 4 cups berries in a buttered baking dish with ½ cup honey and 2 teaspoons lemon juice. Combine ¾ cup dry rolled oats and ½ cup unbleached white or whole wheat flour. Cut in ½ cup butter and sprinkle this mixture over the fruit. Bake in a preheated 375° oven for 35 minutes. This cobbler is good either hot or cold. Top with ice cream, yogurt, or freshly whipped cream.

Mulberry muffins are a feast for the eye as well as the palate. This mulberry-studded bread is made by combining 1 cup unbleached white flour, 1 cup whole wheat flour, 2 teaspoons baking powder, and ½ teaspoon salt. In another bowl mix together 1 egg, ½ cup milk, ¼ cup oil, and ½ cup honey. Combine the liquid and dry ingredients, mixing just enough to moisten—the batter should be lumpy. Now fold in 1 cup of mulberries. Fill 12 oiled muffin cups two-thirds full and bake in a preheated 400° oven for 20 to 25 minutes until golden brown. Turn out of pan as soon as they are done. Like most quick breads, these muffins are best while still warm.

Our main complaint about making wine is that we have to wait so long to enjoy the finished product. If you agree, you will love this mulberry wine. Choose mulberries just beginning to change from red to black. Spread them out on a cloth and leave them there for 24 hours. Then, place the berries in a kettle and force out all the juice with a potato masher or large cooking spoon. Drain off all the juice and discard the berries. For each gallon of juice, boil 1 gallon of water with a few cinnamon sticks. To each gallon of boiling water, add ¾ cup honey, 1 gallon mulberry juice, and 2 cups dry white wine. Pour this mixture into a crock and let stand for 5 or 6 days. (The crock should be covered with a double thickness of cheesecloth or some kind of screen to keep out insects.) The wine can then be put into bottles and is ready to drink any time. Store in a cool place.

The white or Russian mulberry (*Morus alba* var. *tatarica*) is occasionally found in waste places and along fencerows and roadsides scattered throughout the state. The berries are white to pink-purple and are used in the same way as the red mulberry although they are not as sweet.

Nettles

Nettles may not immediately conjure up visions of delectable eating but if given a chance they are just that. In Indiana the Canada nettle (*Laportea canadensis*) can be found throughout the state except in hilly counties, although it isn't actually abundant anywhere. The Canada nettle is strictly a woodland nettle found in wet woods, along streams, and in other moist places. The tall nettle (*Urtica procera*) can be found in the Lake Area but is only occasionally sighted farther south. It prefers rich, porous soil and is restricted mostly to low places around lakes and ponds, in woods, and along unimproved roads. Nettles are most often and most painfully recognized by the sting they inflict if you touch them. Stinging hairs that contain formic acid cover the plant. This erect herb is from two to four feet high with opposite, regularly toothed leaves that are oval, oblong, and strongly veined. Nettles bear greenish flowers.

The leaves are delicious if picked in the spring and early summer while the plant is still young (less than a foot high). Gather nettles with leather gloves and a knife since even this young they can sting. We use kitchen tongs to avoid handling them during preparation. With tongs, hold the nettles under running water until clean. Put into a pot with a tight-fitting lid. Add no water. Steam them gently in the water that clings to the leaves for about 20 minutes. Drain the cooked nettles and reserve the liquid. Season the nettles and serve them with a dollop of yogurt or sour cream garnished with chopped green onion tops. Serve the liquid steaming hot in cups to sip along with the meal.

Nettles are very high in vitamins A and C and were valued by pioneers as a spring tonic. They are highly prized as a vegetable in Europe and the Scots often cultivate them in their gardens. They are assuredly one of our favorite wild greens. We have also used the cooled cooking liquid of nettles for a hair rinse to bring out highlights and combat dandruff. We were pleased with the results and quickly decided that nettles are a beauty aid that works inside and out.

Wild Ginger

Wild ginger (*Asarum canadense* and *A. reflexum*) can be found in the moist, rich soil of woods throughout the state. Ginger prefers shade and likes sheltered situations on wooded slopes or in ravines. Wild ginger spreads by underground stems; thus, it is always found in dense colonies. The velvety leaves, heart-shaped with prominent veins, are about four inches across and give off a pleasant fragrance when bruised. The shy flowers, which bloom in May, are nearly hidden beneath the leaves. Each plant bears one three-lobed, hairy, brownish flower on a short stem that arises from the base of the hairy leafstalks.

The underground stem can be gathered anytime but it is fullest in October. It makes a very good substitute for commercial ginger and may be used whole or dried and ground into powder. While it is fresh, we use it in Chinese recipes calling for ginger root. It is best added by shaving off pieces of it with a vegetable peeler so that it will be tender. Wild ginger doesn't taste exactly like Chinese ginger; nevertheless, it adds a nice flavor. The underground stem is also excellent when candied. First, cut the stems into short pieces and boil them until tender; then cover them with a mixture of ¾ cup honey to every cup of water and boil them until the liquid is thick and syrupy. Pack stems and syrup into hot, sterilized jars and seal with double metal canning lids. The next time you make homemade ice cream, top it with a few tablespoons of this mixture, for a real taste treat. Not only do these candied stems taste good, they are also good for you. Debbie Brinegar keeps some on hand and takes a spoonful for stomach upsets. With medicine this good, you don't mind being ill.

Dock Family

Six species of dock (*Rumex* sp.) are scattered throughout Indiana in waste places and old fields. All species are edible, but it is curly dock (*R. crispus*) that most often finds its way to the table. Curly dock is a dark green plant, usually one to three feet tall, with deep yellow roots. Its oblong leaves are six to twelve inches long with wavy or curled margins. Small greenish flowers borne on tall stalks are replaced in the fall by many rusty brown fruits. These are minute, three-parted, heart-shaped seed wings, each bearing one tiny seed. These rusty brown spikes are very conspicous; often the young dock can be spotted in the spring by the old, erect, dry stalks.

The leaves may be gathered from April through October but are at their best in April and May or early fall. The cool days and cold nights seem to bring out the best in them. The leaves may be eaten raw in salads with a little vinegar and oil dressing and impart a nice lemony flavor. Dock is a rich source of vitamins A and C. Dock can be mixed with dande-lion greens and steamed for 15 minutes or until tender. If the dock is bitter or old, the cooking water should be changed

Curly dock

once or twice. We use cooked dock to make Dock Quiche. A rice shell, a pastry crust, or an oiled casserole may be used as the base. To prepare a rice shell, press 1½ cups of cooked rice and a sprinkling of fresh parsley into a pie pan and bake in a preheated 375° oven for 5 minutes or until dry. For the filling, combine 1 cup cooked, chopped dock, 1 cup sautéed mushrooms and onions, and ¾ cup grated cheese. Put this into the rice shell. Reconstitute ½ cup dry milk powder with 1 cup of water and add 3 beaten eggs, 1 tablespoon flour, and ½ teaspoon each of salt and pepper. Pour over the dock and cheese mixture. Bake in a 350° oven for 35 minutes or until set and browned. This is a quick and easy main dish.

Cooked dock is also good topped with curried white sauce and garnished with hard-boiled eggs and sunflower seeds. To make the sauce, melt 2 tablespoons of butter in a heavy pan. Add 2 tablespoons flour and 2 to 3 teaspoons curry powder. Allow this to brown slightly or your sauce will have a "raw" flour taste. Pour in 2 cups milk and bring to a boil, stirring constantly. Reduce heat and continue stirring until thickened. To make this a curried cheese sauce, just add grated cheese and stir until it is melted.

Eating dock is reported to have caused poisoning in livestock because of the potassium oxalate it contains but we don't feel that there is any danger unless huge quantities are eaten.

Since dock is a member of the Buckwheat Family, a buckwheat-type flour can be made by drying the fruits and grinding them into a flour. Before grinding, be sure to winnow out the chaff that surrounds the dry brown fruits. This flour can be added to any bread recipe. Dockwheat pancakes can be made by replacing ½ of the wheat flour in any pancake recipe with ground dock flour.

A relative of curly dock that makes a tangy salad is field sorrel (*Rumex acetosella*). This abundant weed yields young acid shoots that are pleasant in spring salads. Field sorrel is frequent in the north and south parts of the state but relatively rare in the Tipton Till Plain of central Indiana. The presence of this plant usually indicates impoverished soil. Field sorrel looks like dock except that it is smaller, and its leaves are spear-shaped. It bears the familiar dock fruits. Like dock, it contains potassium oxalate and should be eaten in moderation. This sorrel makes excellent soup and can be used in the same way as the wood sorrels (*Oxalis*). To make Field Sorrel Soup, sauté 1 medium onion, chopped, in oil until translucent. Add 2 cups of chopped sorrel and stir to coat with oil. Pour in 4 cups water and slowly bring to a boil. As soon as it begins to boil, reduce the heat and simmer covered for 15 minutes or until sorrel is very tender. Then add ½ cup sour cream and salt and pepper to taste. Put this in a blender until well mixed. Return to pan and heat gently but do not boil. Serve immediately garnished with croutons.

Lamb's Quarters

Lamb's quarters (*Chenopodium* sp.) is a bluish green plant that is a familiar sight in waste places, along roadsides, and in cultivated areas throughout the state. It is commonly found in potato fields and, if undisturbed, will reach a height of four to five feet. Lamb's quarters is sometimes called common pigweed or goosefoot. The lance-shaped alternate leaves are roughly toothed toward the point with a white dusting on the underside. The shape of the leaves has been described as resembling a quarter of lamb as well as a goose's foot. The leafstalks may be streaked with red although the young stem and very young leaves are usually mealy white. It bears spikes of tiny, greenish flowers. Lamb's quarters is a member of the same family as garden beets and spinach and all fourteen species found in Indiana are edible. It is believed that prior to the introduction of corn prehistoric Indians in Indiana cultivated lamb's quarters as a green and for its seeds. It is high in vitamins A and C and an excellent source of calcium. When less than a foot high, the entire plant can be picked and eaten. When it is taller, gather only the new leaves and tender tops. Lamb's quarters

Lamb's quarters

can be gathered from midspring to frost and, unlike other wild greens, do not become bitter as they mature. The greens may be steamed over low heat for 5–10 minutes, placed on buttered whole wheat toast, and topped with a poached egg. Cover the egg with a thin slice of cheese and put under the broiler just until the cheese melts and is bubbly. This is good at breakfast or anytime.

Potatoes and lamb's quarters combine to make a creamy soup. First, sauté 1 chopped onion in 2 tablespoons of oil until yellow. Add 3 cups water, 1 teaspoon salt, 2 cups diced potatoes, and 2 cups chopped lamb's quarters. Cook for about 20 minutes until tender. Add 1 cup sour cream or one

Rough pigweed

12-ounce can evaporated milk and reheat. Serve with croutons and chopped parsley.

In late summer or fall the minute, dull black seeds may be gathered and cleaned with a fine strainer that allows the seeds to fall through but retains the chaff. The seeds may be eaten raw or roasted in a 350° oven for 45 minutes and then ground into a flour. You can use a blender or even a large pepper grinder to turn the seeds into flour. The Indians mixed the seeds with cornmeal and cooked them as a mush or formed the mixture into little cakes, which were then fried. An Indian-style seed bread can be made by combining ½ cup ground lamb's quarters seeds with ½ cup cornmeal, ¾ cup whole wheat flour, 2 teaspoons baking powder, and a sprinkling of salt. Add 1 tablespoon honey, 1 tablespoon oil, and ½ cup of milk. Form into a ball-shaped loaf on a flat baking sheet and bake in a preheated 350° oven for 25–35 minutes. This is a delicious, coarse-textured bread that is best warm. The seeds are also a very good substitute for poppy seeds.

Rough pigweed (*Amaranthus retroflexus*) and slender pigweed (*A. hybridus*) are similar in appearance to lamb's quarters and are often found growing in the same habitats. These plants have a high iron content and can be used in the same manner as lamb's quarters. We use cooked pigweed to make Amaranthus Dumplings. (Better call it this, since no one will want to eat "pigweed" anything!) Combine 2 cups cooked, drained pigweed with 2 beaten eggs, 2 cups croutons, ¼ cup oil, and ½ teaspoon each of oregano, salt, and sage. Add enough flour to give the mixture a soft biscuit texture and chill for 2 hours. Then wet your hands and shape to form small balls. Put into gently boiling, salted water and cook for 10–15 minutes. Serve with tomato or cheese sauce and sprinkle with grated cheese.

As you will see, once you get used to the animal names, lamb's quarters and pigweed are savory and nutritious vegetables.

Pokeweed

Poke "salad" is one of the few wild foods other than wild rice that appear on the supermarket shelf. You may have seen these canned greens before, especially in the South. They are the young shoots of pokeweed (*Phytolacca americana*). Although pokeweed prefers rich, moist soil, it is very adaptable and grows in all kinds of habitats throughout the state. The abundance of this plant is undoubtedly due to birds, who relish the bitter purple berries, and the fact that grazing animals will not eat it. Rarely occurring in thick stands, pokeweed is a very conspicuous plant which sometimes reaches a height of six to eight feet and has stalks that turn a bright lavender to purple in the autumn. The alternate leaves are five to nine inches long and have a rounded lance shape with wavy margins. Greenish white flowers grow in long clusters opposite the leaves and are replaced by many large purple black berries. Writers cannot seem to agree whether these berries are poisonous or edible. Most contemporary writers list the berries as poisonous, but some very reliable writers of the past write about enjoying pokeberry pies and cobblers after having added vinegar to

the berries. However, we must admit that the ominous-looking berries have never enticed us to settle the argument. The berries do make an excellent ink and we wrote a completely legible letter using this ink and a feather pen. The berries can also be used as a dye.

The huge perennial roots are extremely poisonous, but the many young sprouts that grow from the roots are delicious. The young sprouts are best located either by remembering where the flamboyant fall foliage was or by finding the dried stalks still standing from last year. Spring is the best time to gather the thick young sprouts since the old stems as well as the berries and root are poisonous. When the sprouts first emerge the leaves are tightly curled around the stalk and they resemble asparagus. Soon the leaves unroll and the thick stalk is revealed. The sprouts may be prepared with the center stalk or the leaves and stalk may be prepared separately. The leaves are especially good when fixed with wild mustard greens and served with vinegar and oil. The asparaguslike sprouts can be steamed until tender and served with hollandaise or cheese sauce. They are also good cooked, chilled, and mixed with mayonnaise and chopped boiled eggs. Hoosiers in the southern part of the state dip the sprouts in egg, roll them in cornmeal, and fry them in hot oil or butter. The sprouts are also good when scrambled with eggs. Do not use sprouts that are more than 6–8 inches high.

You may like the poke "salad" or pokeweed so much that you want to freeze it for winter eating. Just boil the sprouts for 10 minutes, drain, and freeze in tightly sealed plastic bags. When the snow falls and winter is all around you, prepare a package of your frozen pokeweed and savor the wild flavor.

Spring Beauty

Spring beauty (*Claytonia virginica*) is a beautiful wild-flower common in moist or dry woods in every county of the state. This delicate plant, which is seldom more than six inches high, bears flowers that are white to pale rose with darker rose veins. The nodding flowers, which seem too heavy for their slender stems, have five petals and five tiny golden stamens. In early spring the flowers often carpet wooded slopes or meadows. The stems nearly always have just two slender, pointed leaves. Several inches below the ground are irregularly shaped, starchy tubers (technically known as corms). When cooked, they taste like a cross between a potato and a chestnut. The Indians highly prized these tubers and eagerly sought them every spring. They are rich in vitamins A and C and when eaten raw have a radishlike taste. The tubers are usually one to two inches in diameter and can be boiled or roasted like potatoes but are easier to prepare if they are cooked in their "jackets." We make Spring Beauty Fondue by first scrubbing the tubers with a vegetable brush and then boiling them unpeeled for 10–15 minutes. The skins are then removed with a sharp knife and the tubers placed on a platter surrounding a dish of hot melted butter. Each person is given a fondue fork so that he or she can spear the beauties and dip them into the butter. This dish will perk up any "wild" party.

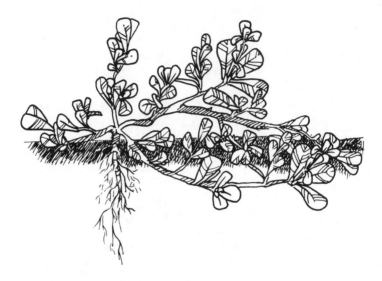

Purslane

Due to its enormous seed production, purslane (*Portulaca oleracea*) is very prolific. It is found in the rich soils of cultivated gardens and fields and in fertile waste places throughout the state. Purslane is a low-lying plant forming mats that are seldom more than one or one-and-a-half inches high. Its fleshy, forking stems are jointed and greenish purple with red tints. The stems radiate from the center of the plant. Narrow thick leaves about two inches long are scattered in nearly opposite positions. The small yellow flowers which open only in sunlight, have five to seven petals and appear on the stem where the stalk forks. The flowers are followed by small, round seed vessels with tops that lift off like lids when ripe. The tiny seeds can be gathered and ground into a meal to be used in bread recipes by replacing one fourth of the wheat flour with seed meal.

Purslane is available from June to September and although you can eat the entire plant, the flower buds, leaves, and branches are best. The best way to gather purslane is to pinch off the leafy tips and wash them well to remove any grit. This plant is good raw and has a watery, acid taste that is very refreshing on a hot day. Since purslane is so thick and succulent, it loses little bulk in cooking and cooks quickly. Drop the purslane into a very small amount of boiling water and let it simmer for about 5 minutes. Serve with green onion sauce and chopped green onions. To make the sauce, melt 2 tablespoons butter in a heavy skillet. Add 2 tablespoons flour and cook slightly. In a blender, combine 2 cups milk with 4 green onions, tops and all. Add this mixture to the flour paste and cook over medium heat, stirring, until thickened.

Purslane is also delicious fixed in a casserole mixed with chopped boiled eggs, sunflower seeds, and white sauce. Top with a layer of wheat germ and bake in a moderate oven for fifteen or twenty minutes. Like okra, purslane has a mucilaginous quality that will thicken soups and stews. Many people use the stems to make pickles that resemble dill pickles. In a hot, sterilized quart canning jar, put a clove of garlic and a dill flower. Pack the jar with fresh purslane stems and cover with a mixture of 1 cup vinegar, 2 cups cold water, ¼ cup salt, and ½ teaspoon of alum. Put into a boiling water bath for 15 minutes. In six to eight weeks they are ready to eat. Young pokeweed sprouts may also be pickled in this manner.

The next time you weed your garden, take the purslane into your kitchen instead of to the compost pile.

Chickweed

Chickweed (*Stellaria media*) is available most of the year and can be found in fields, gardens, waste places, and cultivated areas, as well as in woods and moist places throughout the state. This low-growing plant begins growing in fall, lives through the winter, starts blooming in late winter and by springtime begins going to seed. This cycle is attributed to the fact that chickweed closes its flowers or "sleeps" on cool, dark, cloudy days and at night. It only opens its flowers in sunlight. The much-branched, pale green, sprawling plant has weak, hairy stems that are up to a foot long but seldom rise more than a few inches off the ground. Every few inches on the numerous slender branches are opposite pairs of smooth, oval leaves with sharply pointed tips. The deeply notched flowers have five petals that look more like ten petals at first glance. In spring the seeds appear in papery capsules.

The top stems and leaves are best to eat; older parts are stringy. Chickweed is rich in iron and vitamin C and should be steamed quickly in a small amount of water for only 2–5 minutes or until tender. It can be eaten plain with butter or topped with vinegar and chopped green onions. Because of its mild flavor, chickweed is good cooked with other stronger-tasting greens. Raw, it is a nice addition to salads. A super wild salad is made by combining a variety of crisped greens such as chickweed, dandelion greens and chopped crowns, dock, a little field sorrel (or wood sorrel), and chopped cattail shoots. Add alfalfa sprouts, chopped green onions, sunflower seeds, and chopped black walnuts. For the dressing combine ¼ cup white (or wine) vinegar, and pinches of thyme, marjoram, garlic powder, cumin, and coriander. Put on dressing just before serving this "wild" salad. There are an endless number of combinations that can be used but the addition of wild greens perks up any ordinary salad.

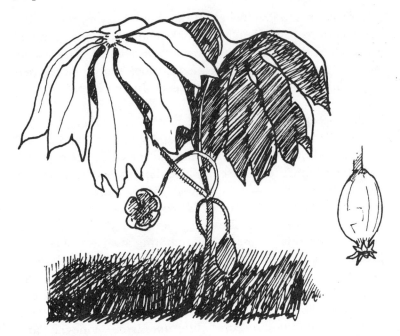

Mayapple

In early spring dense colonies of mayapples (*Podophyllum peltatum*) can be seen in moist woods scattered throughout the state. The dark brown, poisonous rootstalks are horizontal and jointed and remain in the ground year after year, sending up a new plant every spring. The plant pushes its way through the soil, unfolding a pair of large, stalked, umbrellalike leaves on a stalk twelve to eighteen inches tall. The pair of leaves is nearly a foot in diameter. Each leaf has five to seven lobes with two-inch clefts at their ends. There are one-leafed mayapples but they do not bear fruit. A single waxy-white one-inch flower with six to nine petals is suspended in the fork of the leafstalks. The flower appears in May and is followed by a two-inch-long, many-seeded, egg-shaped fruit that ripens from July through September. This slightly acid fruit has a tough skin and in size and color resembles a small lemon. Although sweetly fragrant when ripe, it has a disagreeable odor when green. It is essential to pick only when ripe as the unripe fruit can cause diarrhea and vomiting. The ripe fruit is soft and yellow and will drop into the hand at a touch. The jellylike pulp inside the thick skin can be eaten raw or cooked. Even when ripe, mayapples should be eaten only in moderation to avoid gastric upsets. To prepare mayapples for cooking, wash and cut off the black tips and navels. Slice and run through a colander. If you cook this purée mixed with honey and cinnamon to taste over low heat for 20–30 minutes, you have an excellent mayapplesauce that is good either plain or served with yogurt or ice cream. The purée may also be used to make mayapple marmalade: Boil 4 cups of purée with 1¾ ounces (one box) of commercial pectin for 1 minute. Add 2 tablespoons lemon juice and 4 cups honey and bring to a high boil. Immediately pour into hot, sterilized jars and seal. This makes a thick, orange yellow marmalade.

Another treat is mayapple cake made with mayapplesauce. Combine 2¼ cups whole wheat pastry flour, 1 teaspoon baking soda, ¼ teaspoon salt, 1 teaspoon cinnamon, and ½ teaspoon each of cloves and nutmeg. In a separate bowl beat 1 egg, 1 teaspoon vanilla, 1 cup honey and ½ cup butter until fluffy. Stir in the flour mixture alternately with 1 cup mayapplesauce, beating after each addition. Stir in 1 cup chopped hazelnuts or black walnuts and pour into a well-greased 8 x 8 x 2 inch square pan. Bake in a preheated 350° oven for 35 minutes or until center springs back when lightly touched with fingertip. This cake tastes even better the second day. Serve with freshly whipped cream.

May the mayapple bring a little spring into your fall.

Pawpaw

The pawpaw (*Asimina triloba*) is a small shrub or tree, rarely taller than thirty feet, found in thickets in shady woods and along streams scattered throughout the state although there are fewer pawpaws in the northwest. The smooth, thin bark is dark brown with occasional light patches. The pawpaw, sometimes called Indiana banana, has large tropical-looking leaves and is a member of the tropical Custard Apple Family. The simple alternate leaves are dark green above and lighter beneath with smooth margins. The thin-textured leaves are four to twelve inches long and taper towards the base with short-pointed tips. In late April or May, large solitary flowers, one to one-and-a-half inches wide, are borne on short stalks below the leaves. They are green at first, later turning maroon. The stubby, bananalike fruit, which is three to five inches long, is green at first, turning as it ripens in late August, yellowish to dark brown. The bright yellow pulp contains numerous flat, shiny, brown seeds. The fruit usually falls to the ground when ripe. Pawpaws that are not quite ripe can be left in a dark, dry place to ripen. Like many tropical fruits, they have a flavor that takes some getting used to. Ripe pawpaws are creamy and sweet and can be eaten raw or cooked. They have an almost sickly sweet smell when ripe.

The Indians loved these sweet fruits and harvested them every year. Our Hoosier poet James Whitcomb Riley described the pawpaw as being like a custard pie without a crust.

In the thrill of first discovery, we ate several raw pawpaws, but we have since found we like them best when they are made into pawpaw bread or pie. The pie is made by thoroughly combining ¾ cup honey, ½ cup milk, 2 eggs, ¼ teaspoon salt, and 1½ cups of pawpaw pulp. (Make the pulp by pushing the pawpaws through a colander to remove the seeds and skin, or peel and seed by hand and purée the pulp in a blender until smooth.) Cook this over medium heat until thickened. Then pour the mixture into an unbaked 9-inch pie shell and bake in a preheated 425° oven for 10 minutes, then reduce to 350°, and bake 20–30 minutes more until the crust is nicely browned, and the center is firm. Cool and top with freshly whipped cream or meringue.

To make pawpaw bread, beat ½ cup butter, ¾ cup honey, and 1 egg in a large bowl until fluffy. Mix together 2 cups whole wheat pastry flour, 1 teaspoon baking powder, and ½ teaspoon soda. Stir the flour mixture into the honey mixture alternately with 1 cup mashed pawpaws. Stir in ½ cup chopped walnuts and pour into a well-greased loaf pan. Bake in a preheated 350° oven for 1 hour or until center springs back when lightly pressed with fingertip. Let cool for 5 minutes before turning out of pan. Cool completely before slicing. This bread is especially good spread with a mixture of cream cheese and honey and served with steaming cups of Red Zinger tea.

Pawpaw ice cream tastes exotic but is simple to make. Combine 3 cups of uncooked pawpaw pulp with 5 tablespoons lemon juice, 1 grated lemon peel, 1 cup orange juice, and 1½ cups honey. Whip until fluffy, then stir in 3 cups cream. Pour into a cake pan and freeze. This makes approximately 2 quarts.

Valerie Savage, a wild food plant enthusiast from Bloomington, recommends pawpaws and yogurt as a winning combination. If you are one of those people who fall in love with pawpaws, try baking them in their skins in a 375° oven for 20 minutes. Serve with cream and enjoy the sweet, rich flavor of the pawpaw.

Sassafras

Sassafras (*Sassafras albidum*) is a small tree belonging to the Laurel Family; it forms thickets in dry, sandy loam along borders of woods, along roadsides, and in fence corners throughout the state. Although found in all parts of Indiana, sassafras is most common in southern Indiana, frequent in the western, northwestern, and extreme northern counties, and rare in the east-central part. One of the first cargoes shipped from the American colonies was sassafras. It was highly valued for its deeply furrowed, reddish brown bark, which was used commercially to flavor medicines, to scent perfumes, and to make candy. The Indians and pioneers used the roots to make a spring tonic to "thin the blood." In the early nineteenth century sassafras was a popular spring tonic and there were many sassafras vendors in southern Indiana. According to Ruby Stainbrook Butler, the most famous of these was "Sassafras George," an eccentric peddler named George Adams, who lived in Brown County near Nashville. Old George gathered sassafras roots, put them in a wheelbarrow, and peddled them all over the countryside to Hoosier housewives and to the food markets in Indianapolis. Dressed in shabby clothes and accompanied by tramps and hoboes, Sassafras George could usually be seen trudging down the middle of the road with his wheelbarrow, forcing both autos and horses to go around. His pockets were often stuffed with pawpaws, which he dearly loved. Sassafras George became such a well-known figure that even before his death other sassafras vendors called themselves "Sassafras George." In time the name became synonymous with sassafras vendors in Indiana.

Many people today still adhere to the spring ritual of drinking sassafras tea and, as soon as the ground thaws, gather young roots to boil into a tea. The tea is a rich, beautiful red and two or three brewings can be made from the same root. If older roots are used, the outer bark should be scraped off and shavings made of the root. We drink sassafras tea all year because we like the pungent, spicy flavor. It is delicious iced and makes a great summer drink. The leaves, twigs, bark, and berries all have the distinctive sassafras odor. The tree is easily recognized by its unusual leaves. On the same tree there will be three kinds of alternate leaves. One kind is oval and entire, another is mitten-shaped, and the third has three lobes with the largest lobe in the middle. The young leaves are dried and ground into a powder to make filé, a necessary ingredient in Creole cooking. Because of the mucilaginous quality of the leaves, one tablespoon of filé in a pot of soup flavors and thickens it. The filé should be added just before serving and the soup must not boil again or it will be stringy. Sassafras flowers are greenish yellow and are followed by dark blue one-half inch berries borne on thick red stems. The green buds and twigs are eaten as a spicy nibble.

Sassafras jelly can be made from extra-strength sassafras tea. Put 2 cups of strong tea in a pan and add 1¾ ounces (one box) powdered pectin. Barely bring to a boil and add 3 cups strained honey and 2 tablespoons sassafras root bark grated to a fine powder. Simmer 6 minutes. Put in jelly glasses and immediately cover with melted paraffin.

James Buchanan Elmore, a Hoosier writer, described the qualities of the sassafras very well in the following tribute:

In the Spring of the year, when the blood is thick,
There's nothing so good as a sassafras stick.
It quickens the liver and strengthens the heart
And to the whole system doth new life impart.
Oh sassafras, oh sassafras
Thou art the stuff for me.

If you want to rid yourself of the wintertime blahs, get up early one bright and sunny spring morning, find yourself a woods bordered by sassafras trees, dig the root, and by the time you get home to make the tea, your spring tonic will already be starting to take effect.

Spicebush

Spicebush (*Lindera benzoin*) is a common shrub, six to fifteen feet high, found in the rich, moist soil of damp woods,
ravines, and under tall trees throughout the state. Spicebush
and sassafras are the only two members of the Laurel Family
found in Indiana. In March or April the densely clustered
honey-yellow flowers appear before the leaves. The small,
stalkless, spicy-scented flowers do not have any petals al-

though the six sepals look like petals. The smooth, dark green leaves, three to five inches long, are alternate and oval or oblong with entire edges. The oily, aromatic oval berries that appear in late June or early July are half an inch long and contain one large oval seed. The green berries have a distinct citruslike scent. Although the berries are green at first, they later turn to bright scarlet as they ripen in August through October. The young leaves, twigs, bark, and berries all have a distinctive spicy odor and taste and can be used individually or in combination to make a refreshing tea. Indians and pioneers both drank spicebush tea for its restorative qualities. It was traditional for pioneers to drink it in the spring as a tonic. During the American Revolution the berries were reportedly dried and powdered and used as a substitute for allspice. Although we have never powdered the berries, we often make spicebush tea by brewing a handful of twigs, dried leaves, crushed berries, or bark in 4 cups of water for 15 minutes. This tea smells tantalizing while it is brewing and lives up to the promise of its aroma. We like this tea with lemon or maple syrup. A sprig of spicebush makes an attractive and flavorful stirrer for sassafras tea.

Early settlers considered the spicebush an indication of good farmland. If this is the case, then Spiceland in Henry County must have been fertile since it was named for its abundance of spicebush.

Mustard Family

Black mustard (*Brassica nigra*) is probably one of the most well known of the numerous species of European mustard. This plant is very common in sandy soil throughout Indiana. The sunny yellow flowers sometimes fill entire fields or hillsides from June until September. The finely toothed leaves, four to six inches long, are fuzzy with a covering of tiny, stiff hairs and are borne on slender stems. The larger, lower leaves are the edible ones. These are irregularly shaped, with large terminal lobes and several small lobes at the base of the leaf. These larger leaves, or mustard greens, are an exceptionally good source of vitamins A, B_1, B_2, and C as well as many trace minerals. Mustard greens are at their very best in early spring while the weather is still cool; they may be added raw to salads or cooked alone or in combination with other greens. Since mustard greens cook down a lot, start with twice the volume of leaves you want to end up with and steam for 25–30 minutes. Goldenrod sauce is a bright-colored, delicious topping for the greens. Just boil 3 or 4 eggs and separate the whites from the yolks. Chop the whites and stir them into a white sauce. Pour the sauce over the greens and grate the yolks onto the top.

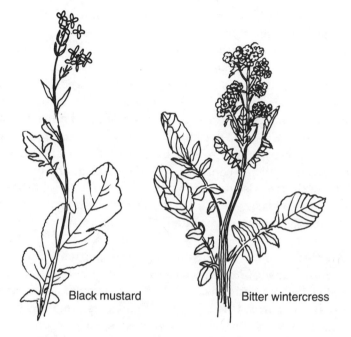

Black mustard   Bitter wintercress

Like all members of the Mustard Family, black mustard has four-petaled flowers, each with six stamens (four long ones and two short ones). When the flat-topped clusters of buds first appear, they resemble small broccoli heads. The flowering top is one to two inches long, with buds spreading out thickly along its length. Eventually the clustered buds develop into cross-shaped yellow flowers. The flowers can be gathered from the time the buds first appear until nearly all the flowers are open. The small leaves that surround the flowers are extremely bitter and should be discarded. The buds may be boiled or steamed for 3–5 minutes, drained, then sautéed in olive oil, and topped with grated Parmesan cheese.

The flowers mature into four-sided pods filled with small seeds that arc good in salads, added to pickles, or mashed and mixed with vinegar to make the familiar condiment mustard. To make dry mustard, pick the entire seed stalk and dry the pods in the sun for several days, until the pods open easily when pounded gently with a wooden mallet. Winnow out the pods and grind the dried seeds in a food chopper or peppermill. Use this powder in any recipe calling for ground mustard, or mix equal parts of dried mustard and unbleached white flower that has been oven-toasted to an even light brown. Add to this a mixture of half vinegar and half water until the consistency is the same as the commercial condiment. Use on sandwiches or as a coating for baked fish. With a pastry brush, coat the fish with mustard and bake uncovered in a preheated 325° oven for 30 minutes or until done.

Another member of the Mustard Family, bitter wintercress or yellow rocket (*Barbarea vulgaris*) bears the familiar four-petaled flowers and is well distributed throughout Indiana. Like all mustards, it is best identified by its tangy taste and crosslike flowers. Bitter wintercress is an early bloomer usually found in colonies along railroads and roadsides, in pastures, and in cultivated fields. Each lustrous green leaf has two or three small, rounded lower lobes and a large terminal lobe. The young flower buds and leaves of bitter wintercress may be used in the same manner as black mustard, although it is essential to pick only young plants to avoid bitterness.

The tender young plants of bittercress (*Cardamine pennsylvanica*) are found in wet or moist soils scattered throughout Indiana. The oblong to oval leaflets of the compound leaves are often toothed, with the terminal leaflet being the largest. The flowers are very small and white, maturing into elliptical seed pods. Bittercress may be gathered from March to June and the young plant may be added to salads or cooked as a green.

Pennycress (*Thlaspi arvense*), a member of the Mustard Family naturalized from Europe, is found scattered

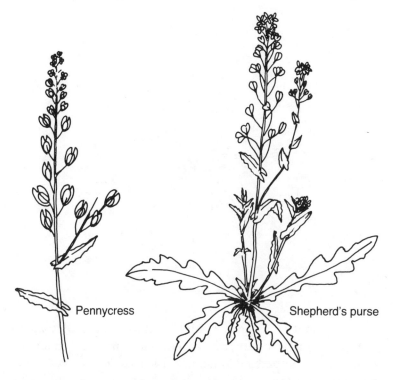

Pennycress

Shepherd's purse

throughout the state. The leaves are arrowhead-shaped with the lobes at the base pointing downwards. The young leaves are good in salads or may be cooked.

Shepherd's purse (*Capsella bursa-pastoris*), four to twenty-four inches tall, is a species of the Mustard Family common the year round in cultivated grounds and along railroads and roadsides throughout the state. Shepherd's purse grows rosettes of long dandelionlike leaves. The tiny white flowers become heart-shaped seed pods. The young greens are good raw or cooked and the taste resembles turnips or cabbage.

From May to July the young shoots of pepper grass (*Lepidium virginicum*) may be found growing all over Indiana except in dense woods or wet places. Pepper grass is

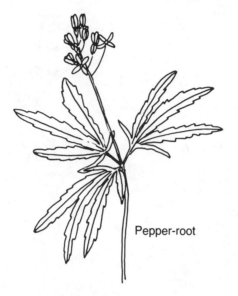

Pepper-root

four to twenty-four inches high and bears small, white, four-petaled flowers. Its smooth, curved stems are branching with deeply toothed spatula-shaped leaves. The leaves are a peppery addition to salads or add spice to soups. The rounded seed pods contain black seeds that can be used as a substitute for pepper.

From April through May, pepper-root or cut-leaved tooth-wort (*Dentaria laciniata*) can be found in rich woods and along the borders of thickets throughout the state. On a stem eight to twelve inches high there is a whorl of three peppery-tasting leaves; each leaf looks something like a hand, being divided into three to five fingerlike segments that are sharply incised. White or purple-tinged flowers in the form of the familiar mustard cross mature into slender, one-inch-long seed pods that are slightly flattened. The crisp peppery roots are a series of small white oval joints that are strung like pop-beads and separate as easily. They can be eaten as a nibble and their pungent taste, like radishes, will complement picnic foods.

Although not common in Indiana, watercress (*Nasturtium officinale*) can sometimes be found in, or at the edges of, running water, springs, and small streams. The succulent leaves have three to nine small oval or oblong leaflets. The leaflet at the end is usually larger than the rest. The small white petals of the flowers are cross-shaped and located toward the tips of the stems. The pungent taste of watercress is excellent in salads or added to sandwiches in place of the condiment mustard. Be *very* sure the watercress is from clean, unpolluted water.

The mustards have the reputation for being a good spring tonic and we agree that the members of this large family are helpful allies that bring health and zest into our lives.

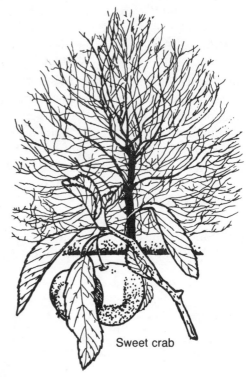

Sweet crab

Crab Apples
and Hawthorns

Wild sweet crab (*Pyrus* or *Malus coronaria*) can be found in various soils of various moistures throughout the state. Sweet crab generally grows in colonies in open woods and clearings and along roadsides and fences. Crabs were probably not very abundant in early Hoosier forests, but the removal of large trees has been favorable to their growth. In addition, crabs are common ornamentals in suburbs and cities. Sweet crab at maturity usually reaches a height of twenty-five feet and has a trunk ten inches in diameter that is deeply furrowed and reddish brown. The twigs often have sharp spines or spurs. The simple alternate leaves are three to four inches long and variable: all have sharply toothed margins, rounded bases, and sharp tips; but some are oval and others are slightly lobed. The sweet-smelling flowers are rosy white, one to two inches across, and five-petaled. The small flower clusters appear in May and are followed by yellow green apples. The hard, sour apples turn red as they ripen in the fall. Although the apples are not very good raw, they can be used to make a delicious jelly or crab apple butter. To make the butter, gather the apples after the first frost but before the ground freezes. Slice the apples in half, barely cover with apple cider or water and simmer until soft. Slightly cool and run through a food mill or colander to remove seeds and core. Put the puréed sauce into a kettle and add honey, cinnamon, ginger, and cloves to taste. It should taste tarter than regular apple butter. Cook over low heat until thickened and a rich burnt-orange color. Pour into hot, sterilized jars and seal.

The crab apple butter can be used to make moist, spicy cookies. First cream together ½ cup butter and ½ cup honey. Add 1 beaten egg to this mixture and blend thoroughly. In another bowl combine 2 cups whole wheat flour, ½ teaspoon salt, ½ teaspoon soda, and 1 teaspoon baking powder. Add the dry ingredients to the creamed mixture alternately with 1 cup crab apple butter. Be sure to make the flour the first addition and the last. If desired, fold in 1 cup chopped nuts or raisins. Drop by teaspoonfuls onto a well-oiled cookie sheet. Bake in a preheated 375° oven for 12–15 minutes. This should make about 2 dozen cookies.

Miniature crab apples pickled whole are an attractive relish. Gather 8 quarts of crab apples that are of a uniform size. Wash and remove the blossom ends but do not peel. Tie 6 cinnamon sticks and ¼ cup whole cloves together in a cheesecloth bag. Put 1 quart vinegar, 4 cups honey, and the spice bag into a pan and heat to boiling. Add the crab apples

Hawthorn

and reheat slowly so that the skins do not break. Simmer gently until the apples are tender. Then pack the apples into hot, sterilized canning jars, cover with the syrup, and seal. This yields about 8 to 10 pints. These bright little apples are great for holiday meals.

As you will see, these bite-sized apples are only "crabby" until you get to know them. Handled properly, they can be sweet and delicious.

Similar to the sweet crab is the prairie crab (*P. ioensis*), a low, wide-spreading tree restricted to the western part of the state referred to as the Prairie Area. Although the sweet crab is woolly when young, the leaves and branch ends of prairie crab are even woollier and downier. The prairie crab is similar to the sweet crab in other respects and can be used in the same manner.

A close relative of the crab is the hawthorn (*Crataegus* sp.), which also bears an applelike fruit used primarily for jelly making. Of the twenty-seven species of hawthorn found in pastures, thickets, and borders of woods scattered throughout Indiana, the four most common species are the cockspur thorn (*C. crus-galli*), the red haw (*C. mollis*), sugar haw (*C. calpodendron*), and the dotted haw (*C. punctata*). Although it is hard to tell the varieties apart, the hawthorn group is easily recognized by its stiff thorns, which appear on crooked branches bearing oblong or oval leaves. The apple-red fruits are preceded by clusters of five-petaled white flowers. The fruit contains one to five hard seeds; its edible yellow flesh ripens in September. Some trees bear better haws than others. If you find a good source, try making this spicy haw jam. Simmer 1½ quarts of haws, barely covered with water, until soft. Put the softened haws through a colander. In a large pot, combine 4 cups fruit purée, 4 cups honey, ½ cup apple juice, and 3 teaspoons apple pie spice. Simmer until thickened. Pour into hot jelly jars and seal. We like this jam on hot English muffins that have been thickly spread with cream cheese.

Another good use of haws is Haw Wine. In the fall, pick 6 pounds of ripe haws. Wash well and cut off the stalks. Put them in a crock and pour in a gallon of boiling water. With a wooden spoon, stir and mash well. Cover and let stand for 10 days, stirring daily. After 10 days, strain and add 3 pounds of turbinado sugar. Stir until all the sugar has dissolved, then cover and leave for 4 more days. Stir daily. Now the wine is ready to bottle. Cork loosely at first since the fermentation will explode the bottles if they are corked too tightly. As the fermentation slows down, push the corks in tighter. This wine is ready to drink in 6 months but it will improve with age. Most of the sugar is consumed during the fermentation process so you don't have to worry about getting an overload of sugar when drinking this wine.

Juneberries

The juicy, blueberrylike fruits of the juneberry (*Amelanchier* sp.), also called serviceberry, sarvis tree, shadbush, and shadblow, were relished by Indians and pioneers alike. Although three species of juneberry or serviceberry are found in Indiana, few Hoosiers make use of this delectable wild fruit. Downy juneberry (*A. canadensis*) is found in dry soil on banks of streams and on wooded slopes sparsely scattered throughout the state. Low juneberry (*A. humilis*) grows in colonies in very sandy soil in woods and along fencerows and roadsides in northern Indiana. Smooth juneberry (*A. laevis*) is found in the Lake Area and can be found scattered throughout Indiana, although it is less common in the southern part and absent from central Indiana. It is frequent on the high dunes facing Lake Michigan and can be found in tamarack bogs, in interdunal flats, and on the low and high banks of lakes and streams. The smooth juneberry is the largest of the three and often is forty feet high with a trunk seven inches in diameter. All three species are similar and tend to hybridize; it is often hard to tell them apart. They prefer dry, sandy soil but will adapt to other kinds readily. As a result the tree will vary in size from a scrubby shrub to a small tree. The shape of the leaves will vary slightly and so will the size and color of the fruit. Generally, the simple alternate leaves are three to four inches long, egg-shaped, and sharply pointed with finely toothed margins. The hairy leaves are borne on slender stems. The bark is smooth and gray with occasional streaks of black. The five-petaled flowers form drooping white clusters, three to five inches long, that appear in the early spring when the leaves are just beginning to open. The berries are red when they first appear and later turn reddish purple to purplish black in June through July as they ripen. Juneberries look somewhat like blueberries. However, juneberries grow in bunches at the top of the tree and you have to bend the branches to reach them. The berries contain soft seeds that can be eaten right along with the fruit. The seeds soften even more when cooked and enhance the flavor.

The berries may be eaten raw or cooked into pies, added to breads or pancakes, or stewed. To stew juneberries, barely cover them with water, add honey to taste, and simmer until soft and thickened. Try this on top of ice cream for a hot juneberry sundae. The stewed fruit can also be used for juneberry shortcake, which we call Debbie Berninger's Delight. Make the biscuits by combining 2 cups wheat flour, ½ teaspoon salt, and 4 teaspoons baking powder. Cut in 4 tablespoons butter. Mix together ¾ cup milk and 2 tablespoons honey and add to the dry ingredients. Knead 20–25 times on a lightly floured board, roll out ½-inch thick, and cut with a floured biscuit cutter into 12–14 biscuits. Place the biscuits in greased pans and bake in a preheated 450° oven for 10–12 minutes until golden brown. Split while hot and top with stewed juneberries and fresh cream. This dessert is equally good when chilled and topped with whipped cream.

Juneberries may be frozen, canned, or dried for winter use. To dry, spread the berries out between wire screens to dry in the sun for several days. Stir occasionally. The berries may also be dried in a slow oven for several hours. The dried fruits may be used like raisins or currants. These dried juneberries are especially good in Juneberry Oatmeal Bread. Bring 2 cups of water to a boil and add 1½ cups old-fashioned rolled oats. Cook 5 minutes, then add ¼ cup soft butter. Turn into a bowl and add 1 cup milk, ½ cup honey, and 1 tablespoon salt. Cool to lukewarm, then beat in 1 egg and 1 package dry yeast. Let stand for 10 minutes until it is bubbly. Now add ½ cup dried juneberries and 5 cups unbleached white flour, 1 cup at a time. Turn out on a floured board and knead for 8–10 minutes until smooth and elastic. Put in a bowl, cover with a clean towel, and place in a warm area for 1 hour or until doubled in bulk. Punch down and knead again. Divide the dough and shape into two loaves. Place the shaped loaves in well-oiled bread pans and let rise for ½ hour. Bake the raised loaves in a preheated 350° oven for 40–45 minutes until they are well-browned and sound hollow when gently thumped. Turn out of the pans and brush the tops with melted butter. Although everyone enjoys hot yeast bread, it will slice better if allowed to cool first.

We think that juneberries are a fruit that Hoosiers have neglected too long. People sometimes forget the simple pleasures of their ancestors.

Pasture rose

Roses

Whether it is a garden rose or a rambling wild rose, the rose (*Rosa* sp.) is held in high esteem for its beauty. However, few people realize that this lovely flower is also a source of delicious food. Besides cultivated roses, there are eight species of wild roses that form thickets along roadsides and in old pastures throughout the state. Roses are shrubby, prickly plants with alternate, pinnate leaves. The most common rose in Indiana is the pasture rose (*Rosa carolina*).

The pink or red solitary flowers borne on panicles have five petals and five sepals and bloom from June to August. The petals are delicious in salads or sandwiches or can be used to make jelly or rose water. Pick only those roses that you are sure have not been sprayed and are free from fungus or insects. The white base of the petals is bitter and must be removed. To do this, grasp several petals between your thumb and forefinger and snip off with scissors. The petals are sweet and colorful tossed into a salad. Rose sandwiches can be made by mixing the petals with melted butter. (Leave the rose butter in the refrigerator for two or three days before using.) Spread the rose butter generously on whole wheat bread, add thinly sliced peeled cucumbers, alfalfa sprouts, and another slice of bread. This makes a nice summer brunch served with assorted raw vegetables and lemonade.

The rosebuds can be pickled by packing them into sterilized jars and covering with a boiling mixture of 2 cups honey, 2 cups vinegar, and 2 cups water. Seal and store for a couple of months; then use in salads or as a relish.

We make rose pancakes by adding petals to the batter and serving rose hip syrup with the pancakes. Rose hips are the reddish orange "fruit" that appears in the fall. They are the fleshy, swollen tips of the flower stalks and, technically, are not really fruit. The real fruits, which many people mistake for seeds, are found inside the pulpy hips. The tasty, sour hips are high in vitamin C, phosphorus, and iron. To make rose hip syrup, barely cover with water hips that have had the blossom ends cut away, and boil until soft. Strain off the juice, reserving it, and boil the hips a second time. Combine the two juice extractions and add ¾ cup honey for every two cups of juice. Boil until thickened, pour into hot, sterilized jars, and seal. This is good on ice cream as well as pancakes.

The hips may be used for tea either fresh or dried. If fresh, chop up and steep to desired strength. To dry, cut away the blossom end and cut them in half. Then let them dry in the sun between wire screens for several days or put them in a 200° oven until crisp. Some roses are better than others and the only way to find a good stand is to taste the hips until you find some good ones. If you find some nice fleshy ones, they can be used to make this old-fashioned rose hip jam. Weigh the rose hips and use 1 cup water for each pound of hips. Simmer covered for 20 minutes until softened and then press through a colander. For each pound of pulp add ¾ cup honey and ground cloves and cinnamon to taste. Simmer until thickened, remembering that it will thicken more when cool. Pour into hot, sterilized jars and seal. Spread on whole wheat muffins fresh from the oven, this jam will brighten up any winter morning.

Rose festivals are held every year in Indianapolis, Michigan City, and Richmond. Richmond, the "City of Roses," is the home of the largest producers of cut roses in the United States.

Wild Strawberry

To the Potawatomie Indians the month of June was known as the moon of the strawberries or "heart-berries," and Indians as well as pioneers sought the tiny red berries. Pioneers were pleased to find that the New World strawberries were more vigorous and abundant than their European counterparts. If you have ever seen a commercial strawberry, you will have no trouble identifying the wild strawberry (*Fragaria virginiana*). This low, spreading plant has three coarsely toothed leaflets borne on a hairy, slender stalk and flowers with five white round petals borne on a leafless stalk. The flowers precede miniature red berries that are smaller than commercial strawberries but much sweeter. Most people do not realize that strawberries are not really fruits any more than the rose hips are fruit. They aren't really berries either. The real strawberry fruits are the "seeds" seen on the surface. However, we still call them berries although botanically this is incorrect. Wild strawberries are found in wet and dry soils in sunny places on open wooded slopes, in crevices of cliffs, along roadsides, in fallow fields, in marshes, and along the right-of-way of railroads throughout the state. The leaves can be used dried or fresh to make a tea that is rich in vitamin C. The flavor of this tea will be enhanced if you brew it with fresh or dried orange peel.

The sweet berries are used in the same manner as cultivated strawberries and make excellent jams. Since the berries are very small, it is tedious to gather them in quantity. We usually eat them as we pick or save a cupful to add to yogurt. A delicious fruit smoothy can be made by combining 1 cup wild strawberries, 1 banana, and 1 cup apple juice. Put in a blender until smooth. This is a thick, sweet drink.

When we do manage to collect a good many berries, we make strawberry roly-poly. To prepare, beat 1 egg, 1 tablespoon honey, and ¼ cup butter until fluffy. Add 1 cup milk and 1 cup flour mixed with 2 teaspoons baking powder. Roll out to form a square and place in a buttered 8 x 8 x 2 inch square pan. Fill with 2 cups of sweetened, mashed berries mixed with 2 tablespoons flour. Pull the four corners together and pinch to seal. Bake in a preheated 400° oven for 30 minutes or until browned and puffed. Serve hot with sweet cream or cold with whipped cream. This is well worth the effort it takes to gather all those tiny berries.

The tiny wild strawberries look their prettiest and taste the sweetest when they are served whole in tarts. To make 8 strawberry-cheese tarts, beat together 3 ounces cream cheese and ⅓ cup whipping cream until stiff and smooth. Line the tart shells with this mixture and add whole strawberries. Mash enough berries to make ½ cup of liquid. Combine this with 1½ tablespoons arrowroot, ⅓ cup honey, and ¼ cup boiling water. Cook, stirring constantly, over medium heat until thickened and clear. Pour over the berries, chill, and serve with whipped cream. Any pastry recipe may be used to make the tart shells but the following is an especially good one. Cut 1 cup of chilled butter into 2 cups unbleached white or whole wheat pastry flour. Add just enough ice water to hold the ingredients together, approximately ½ cup. The dough will be easier to work with if it is first chilled for 2–4 hours. Roll out the pastry to a thickness of ¼ inch. Cut into rounds large enough to fit over the cups of an inverted muffin pan. Bake in a preheated 450° oven for 10–15 minutes until browned. Remove from pan and allow to cool before filling.

Red Raspberry, Black Raspberry, Blackberry, and Dewberry

Few people are strangers to the delight of the berry patch. The wild berries, although smaller, are so much sweeter than commercial berries that most people at one time or another have gone berry-picking. Red and black raspberries, as well as blackberries, are native to America and Indians were quite familiar with this delicious food. Today there are Hoosier fishermen who believe that the time to catch catfish is when the raspberries are ripe. The red raspberry (*Rubus idaeus* var. *strigosus*) is a prickly shrub found throughout the Lake Area. The bristly canes are two to five feet long with a light, powdery-white overcast and bear alternate compound leaves, each with three to five saw-toothed leaflets. The leaflets, green above and white below, are covered with fine hairs. The light red, juicy berries that ripen in July are preceded by greenish white flowers.

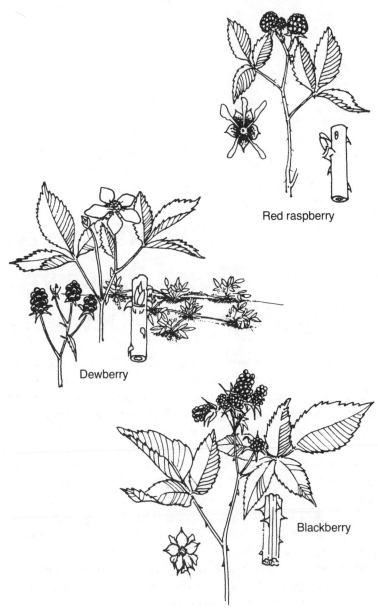

Red raspberry

Dewberry

Blackberry

The black raspberry (*R. occidentalis*) is more common, being found in every county of the state in all kinds of habitats, although it prefers moist soil. The thin, curved canes, six to eight feet long with strong hooked prickles and a heavy white overcast, root at their tips and form impenetrable briar patches. Although the compound leaves usually have three double-toothed leaflets similar to those of the red raspberry, there are occasionally five leaflets.

The blackberry (*R. allegheniensis*) is abundant throughout the state and can be found in all kinds of habitats although it prefers open areas along roadsides, old fields, and other waste places. The erectly arching canes are angular rather than round, extremely prickly, three to seven feet long, and reddish or purple when older. The leaflets are borne in threes or fives and are soft and hairy underneath. The white flower clusters are also hairy. The firm black berries are oblong and composed of many small drupelets. The berries are ripe in July.

The dewberry (*R. flagellaris*) is very similar to the blackberry except that its canes are round, and trailing rather than upright. The stems are several feet long with stout prickles. Each compound leaf has three to seven leaflets. The dewberry is found only in slightly acid soils and is frequent in fallow fields in the Lake Area and southern Indiana. The black fruit is ripe from the last of June to the first of August.

All four kinds of berries can be used interchangeably and may be used in any recipe calling for commercial raspberries or blackberries. The berries are low in pectin and require the addition of commercial pectin to make jam or jelly. To make a sugarless berry preserves, cook 3 quarts of washed berries in a covered pan over low heat until they are well cooked. Boil until thickened slightly. Add 4 cups of apple cider and continue boiling uncovered. Add 1¾ ounces of powdered pectin and continue boiling until thick. Pour into hot, sterilized jars and seal with double metal canning lids. Process in a hot water bath for 5 minutes. Then screw the bands down tightly. This has a rich berry taste with just a hint of apple.

Most people do not need to be told that the berries make excellent cobblers and pies. A pie that is different from the usual double-crust pie can be made by first mashing enough berries to make 1 cup. Then blend 3 tablespoons arrowroot, ⅔ cup honey, and the cup of crushed berries in a small saucepan. Add ½ cup boiling water and cook, stirring constantly, over medium heat until thickened and clear. Cool. Place 1 quart of cleaned and hulled raspberries, blackberries, or dewberries in an 8-inch baked pie shell and pour the thickened sauce over them. Chill and serve topped with whipped cream. This pie is sweet and light and retains all the flavor of the berries.

Any of the berries may be dried and stored for winter use, but blackberries are usually the best because they are large and firm. To dry, put a single layer of berries in a 150° oven for 20 minutes. Then spread between screens and let them dry in the sun for three to ten days. Whenever drying fruits or vegetables, it is a good idea to bring them inside each night to protect them from temperature changes and night marauders. After the berries are thoroughly dried, put them into dry, sterilized jars and seal tightly. The berries may be reconstituted by soaking them in water overnight. Then use them as you would fresh berries, or stew them and serve them plain or as a sauce for cake, pudding, or ice cream. The wild berries are truly one of nature's greatest bounties.

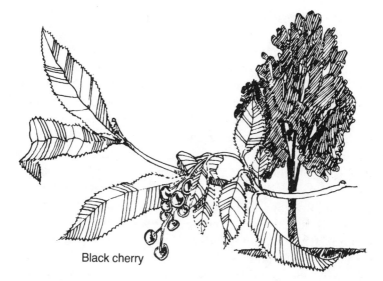

Black cherry

Wild Cherries and Plums

Black cherry (*Prunus serotina*) is a large tree found in open woodlands and along fences and roadsides throughout the state. The alternate simple leaves are thick, shiny, and oblong to lance-shaped; they are two to six inches long with saw-toothed edges and prominent midribs that are hairy on the underside of the leaf. Black cherry, like all cherry and plum trees, has bark characterized by many horizontal streaks. The older cherry bark is dark and rough and the branches are reddish. White flowers appear in early spring when the leaves are half grown. The fruit is dark red at first but turns black or dark purple as it ripens in August and September. The juicy, bitter-sweet cherries are borne in long clusters and resemble grapes. They are best when the tree grows in open sunlight.

Pioneers loved to make cherry-rum cordials by pressing out the juice and mixing it with rum. This drink tasted bitter but was evidently popular enough to make the cherries known as rum cherries in some areas. To extract the juice, barely cover 4 pounds of black cherries in water, cover, and simmer 15–20 minutes. Mash the cherries with a potato masher to get out all of the juice. Strain through a double thickness of cheesecloth and use as desired. For a nice wine-flavored jelly, combine 3 cups of juice, 3 cups mild-flavored honey, and 3½ cups turbinado sugar. (When we try to use all honey in jelly recipes, we sometimes end up with syrup instead of jelly. Usually it works; try using all honey if you want. If nothing else, the syrup is great on pancakes and ice cream. On the other hand, you could use all sugar if you prefer.) Bring the juice mixture to a boil and add one 6-ounce bottle of liquid pectin. Bring to a full, rolling boil, stirring constantly. Boil for 1 minute, immediately remove from heat, and skim off the foam. Pour into hot, sterilized jars and seal with paraffin. This makes 4 or 5 pints.

The common chokecherry (*P. virginiana*) is found in moist woods and along streams and fencerows throughout the Lake Area. Chokecherry is a shrub or small tree seldom taller than twenty feet. The thin, oval leaves, two to four inches long, are sharply pointed and have finely toothed margins. When the leaves are full-grown, clusters of white flowers appear; the dark red pea-sized fruit ripens in July through August. The small cherries are astringent and puckery when raw but become bland when cooked. Chokecherry jelly can be made by following the directions for black cherry jelly. Another very good jelly can be made by mixing the cherry juice half and half with apple or crab apple juice. Chokecherry-Apple Jam is delicious, too. Peel, core, and chop 3½ cups of apples. Cook in a small amount of water until

Chokecherry

soft, then purée them in a blender. Remove the pits from 1 cup of chokecherries. (If the pits are hard to get out, just boil the cherries a minute or two; then the pits will pop out easily.) Combine the applesauce, cherries, 2 cups honey, 1 tablespoon lemon juice, and 2 teaspoons cinnamon. Boil this mixture until thickened. Pour into hot, sterilized jars and seal with paraffin.

A cherry cornbread like that the Indians made can be prepared by first simmering 1 cup of whole chokecherries in 2 cups of water for 20 minutes. Drain the juice from the cherries and reserve the liquid. Pit the cherries by gently squeezing them until the pits pop out. Combine the pitted cherries with 2 tablespoons honey. Grease a 9-inch black iron skillet and put it into a 375° oven to heat while you mix the cornbread. To make the cornbread, combine 1 cup cornmeal, 1 cup whole wheat flour, 2 teaspoons baking powder, and 1 teaspoon salt. Add 1 egg, 1 tablespoon honey, and 2 tablespoons melted butter. Measure the cherry liquid and add enough water to make ¾ cup. Add to other ingredients and stir in sweetened cherries. Pour the batter into the hot skillet and bake for 20–25 minutes. Serve in wedges topped with whipped butter.

Sand cherry (*P. pumila*) is a low bush growing in sandy places and in Indiana is found primarily on the slopes of the dunes facing Lake Michigan. In any recipe calling for black or chokecherries, sand cherries can be substituted. When eating any of these cherries raw, do *not* eat the pits; they contain cyanide. The cyanide is destroyed by thorough cooking.

Pin cherry or fire cherry (*P. pennsylvanica*) is a shrub or small tree occasionally found in the northern tier of the northwestern counties. It prefers wet woodlands, old tamarack bogs, and interdunal swamps. It has narrow leaves and is similar to the black cherry in appearance. The smooth, red brown trunk has horizontal cracks in it. The white flowers appear in umbrellalike clusters. The bright red fruits, which look like miniatures of the familiar pie cherries, are ripe in late summer or early autumn; these cherries are extremely sour when raw and are best used to make a tart jelly. Follow the recipe given for black cherries.

Another member of the Prunus genus is the American plum (*P. americana*), a small tree frequent throughout the state. In Indiana the trunk of the plum rarely exceeds eight inches in diameter, and is usually only two to five inches. The tree is somewhat thorny and has thick, shaggy bark. Plum trees prefer moist soil and form thickets in open woodland, along streams, ponds, and lakes, and in moist prairie habitats. In early April fragrant clusters of three to five small, white, five-petaled flowers appear before the leaves. Flowering plums are nearly always surrounded by large numbers of bees. The three- to four-inch-long leaves are borne on crooked branches. The wrinkled, oblong leaves have sharply toothed margins and many veins. Small round

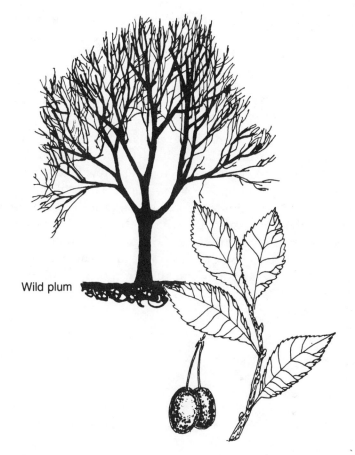

Wild plum

fruits, red or yellow with a white overcast, appear in August. Wild plums are very tangy and tough-skinned but excellent for jams and jellies.

The woollyleaf plum (*P. lanata*), which is frequent along the Ohio River Valley counties of southwestern Indiana and infrequent to rare northward, is similar to the American plum except that it has hairy twigs and leaves. The Canada plum (*P. nigra*) is a very small species found in wet woodlands in the northern half of the state. Its pinkish flowers, which appear in early April, make the tree very conspicuous. There are a few other species of plums in Indiana but they are of less significance.

These small trees do well as long as they are not over-topped and shaded out by taller trees. Many plum trees growing in the wild either do not bear fruit or bear fruit that is diseased or insect-ridden. However, wild plum jam is so delicious that it is worth the effort to find a tree that bears fruit. The jam is very simple and easy to make. Clean 1 pound of wild plums and cook in 1 cup water until the skins are tender, 10–15 minutes. Cool and remove the seeds. Add ¾ pound honey and heat slowly until the honey is absorbed. Then cook rapidly until thick. Cool slightly, stirring occasionally. Pour into hot, sterilized jars and seal. This makes 1–2 cups of jam. The jam will thicken more readily if prepared in small batches like this.

Alfalfa and Clover

Alfalfa (*Medicago sativa*) is a vitamin- and mineral-rich plant that could easily replace your commercial vitamin pills. It is an excellent source of iron, magnesium, phosphorus, sulphur, sodium, potassium, silicon, and vitamins A, D, and K. A persistent escape that is frequent throughout the state, alfalfa is planted for grazing and fodder. The one to one-and-a-half-foot plant, which is available from spring to early summer, has trifoliate leaves. Its typical cloverlike flowers are blue or violet and borne on small spikes. Small twisted pods mature after the flowers.

Dried alfalfa leaves and flower tops make a healthy tea that builds cells and is slightly laxative. To dry, tie the plants in bundles and suspend from the ceiling of a warm, dry room away from sunlight until the leaves are dry enough to be crumbled into a powder. The leaves may be used alone or mixed with equal amounts of spearmint and steeped in boiling water for 10 minutes. The powder may also be sprinkled into soups, juices, or oatmeal but the taste takes some getting used to. We have made alfalfa bread by substituting 1 cup alfalfa flour for 1 cup wheat flour in a tradi-

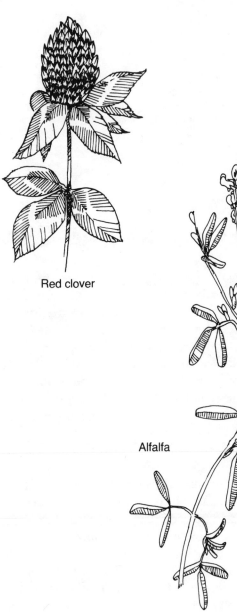

Red clover

Alfalfa

tional 6-cup yeast bread recipe. (The flour is made by whirring the crumbled leaves in a blender until fine.) The resulting bread smelled like a freshly mowed hay field and was pale green. Once we grew accustomed to its unusual taste, we enjoyed eating this healthful bread.

Red clover (*Trifolium pratense*) is also planted for fodder and is frequent along roadsides throughout the state. The blossoms should be picked before they turn brown and dried to use in tea either alone or with mint. Indians drank red clover tea in springtime as a blood purifier. A concoction of red clover tea, onion juice, and strained honey was considered an excellent cough medicine. Pioneers used extra-strength clover tea to relieve the coughing spasms of whooping cough.

White clover (*T. repens*), found throughout the state, is common in lawns, waste places, and pastures. This native of Eurasia has become widely naturalized in North America. The sweet white blossoms are used to make tea. The young leaves of both red and white clover are good on sandwiches or added to tossed salads.

Why not give alfalfa and clover a chance to rejuvenate your sagging spirits?

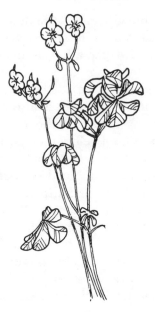

Sorrels

Yellow wood sorrel and violet wood sorrel are the most commonly found sorrels in Indiana. Yellow wood sorrel (*Oxalis stricta*) prefers impoverished soil and grows in abandoned fields and along roadsides and railroads throughout the state, but it is most abundant in the southern counties. The grayish green, cloverlike leaves have a sour-lemon taste and are borne at the ends of long leafstalks that alternate on thin, watery stems. The compound leaves are composed of three leaflets shaped like inverted hearts; the notch at the outer edge often makes a single leaflet look like two overlapping leaflets. The bright yellow flowers have five petals and five sepals.

Violet wood sorrel (*O. violacea*) is found in dry, sandy or clay soils along roadsides and the borders of woods throughout the state except in the northeastern counties. Violet wood sorrel is similar to yellow wood sorrel but violet wood sorrel has a scaly bulblike base, bears violet flowers, and its leaflets are reddish on the underside. Both sorrels are available from late spring through fall. Their leaves are an excellent and refreshing nibble because they are so watery. They also give a nice lemon flavor to tossed salad, cole slaw, or cottage cheese. An excellent omelet filling is made by combining cottage cheese, chopped sorrel, and sunflower seeds. A lemonadelike drink can be made by steeping the leaves in hot water, then sweetening to taste and serving over ice. Sorrel leaves contain oxalic acid so it is important to eat them only in moderation.

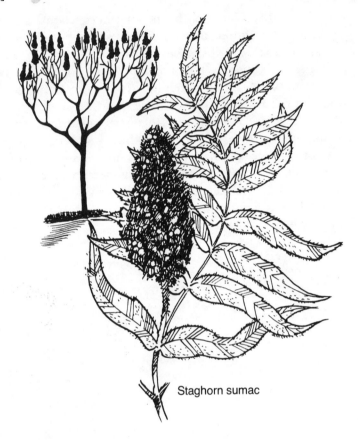

Staghorn sumac

Sumacs

Staghorn sumac (*Rhus typhina*), a shrub or small tree found scattered throughout the Lake Area, forms thickets in neglected fields and along roadsides, railroads, fences, and the borders of woods. This member of the Cashew Family grows rapidly but is short-lived. Its shiny green bark is smooth between the characteristic raised cross streaks, but the young twigs and leafstalks have a dense covering of velvety hairs. The twenty-inch-long, alternate compound leaves are divided into eleven to thirty-one pointed, finely toothed leaflets, each three to five inches in length. The oblong to lance-shaped leaflets are dark green above and pale beneath. Large spikes of small, greenish white or greenish yellow flowers rise above the fronds of foliage; the flowers mature into compact fruit clusters called stags, which are composed of hard red berries rich in malic acid and covered with a bright red fuzz. The hairy-stemmed stags are ripe in late summer.

The stags are used to make a bright red, lemonadelike drink. Although stags may be picked after they have remained on the tree through the winter, it is better to pick them as soon after they ripen as possible since they are very prone to insect infestation. (We have tried picking the stags when they were first turning red, in late June, but the resulting drink was quite bitter.) To make this tart juice, put the ripe stags in water to cover; rub and squeeze between your hands to extract the bright red juice. Strain carefully through a cheesecloth to remove the tiny hairs. Sweeten if desired, add a sliced lemon, and serve over ice. Not only is this a refreshing drink, but it is also a very effective cure for mouth sores. The Potawatomie Indians used sumac juice for this purpose and from our own experience we can vouch for its immediate effectiveness. We gather the heads and dry them for winter use because we enjoy the taste and like to keep this excellent medicine on hand. Supposedly, sumacade can be drunk to counteract a craving for tobacco but since we are nonsmokers, we cannot verify this. We also use the sumac juice to make sumac pie. Combine 1¼ cups sumac juice with ⅓ cup honey, 2 tablespoons butter, and a sprinkling of salt. Put this mixture into a double boiler and add 4 tablespoons cornstarch dissolved in ¼ cup water. Cook until thickened, then add 2 beaten egg yolks. Cook again, stirring constantly, for 2 minutes. Remove from heat and cool completely; then fold in 2 stiffly beaten egg whites. Pour into a baked 9-inch pie shell and chill. Serve topped with freshly whipped cream.

The Indians used the hollow stems for flutes. Sumac is rich in tannic acid and is used in tanning leathers. Since sumac-tanned leather is less likely to decay, it has been used in bookbindings and other fine work where durability is important.

Although staghorn sumac is most commonly used to make sumacade, the smooth sumac (*R. glabra*) and the shining sumac (*R. copallina*), both of which are found in Indiana, can also be used. We have used smooth sumac and can attest to its excellence. Smooth sumac is found scattered throughout the state and is very similar to staghorn sumac except that its leafstalks and twigs are hairless and its leaves are more coarsely serrate. The shining sumac is frequent in the northwestern and southern counties but rare elsewhere in the state. Its leaves have smooth, untoothed margins and there are thin projections or wings along the stems between successive pairs of leaflets. Otherwise it resembles staghorn sumac.

Although these three sumacs are relatives of poison sumac (*R. vernix*), there is very little danger of getting the poison sumac by mistake since it is not found in the same habitat as the other three. Poison sumac prefers a swampy, boggy habitat and its berries are white and form very loose clusters.

Sugar Maple

It was a festive time for the Miami Indians when they returned from their winter hunting grounds with furs and maple syrup and sugar. Not only did they relish this natural sweet but it was also an important item of barter for them. Hoosier pioneers quickly learned from the Indians how to tap the sugar maple (*Acer saccharum*) and make the delicious "tree molasses." In 1900, Indiana ranked third in the nation for production of maple syrup. Today the many sugar camps have all but disappeared but the trees are still abundant for those who care to tap the trees for their cider-colored syrup.

The sugar maple is a wide-spreading forest tree found in rich, well-drained uplands throughout the state. The gray or brownish scaly bark has flat vertical ridges. The simple opposite, three- to five-lobed leaves are borne on long stalks. The leaves are dark green above and lighter beneath with irregular, widely spaced coarse teeth that are sharply pointed. When the leaves are unfolding, clusters of small greenish yellow flowers on drooping stalks appear at the base of the leafstalks. The fruits are one- to one-and-a half-inch seeds that have long wings. The fruits are suspended in pairs from a long, single stalk. These fruits may be gathered in autumn and make a nice nibble, especially when roasted and buttered. Remove the wings and roast the seeds in a 250° oven until they are crisp, usually 20–30 minutes. Add butter and salt and eat like popcorn. The seeds may also be boiled and eaten with butter and milk.

The best time for tapping the sap is from January to spring when there are warm sunny days and cold nights. This temperature change is what makes the sap "run." So as not to damage the tree, it is wise to tap only those trees that have a diameter of ten to twelve inches. One large tree should yield about a gallon of syrup a year and it takes thirty to forty gallons of sap to make one gallon of syrup. The sap may be drunk directly from the tree or used in cooking but its true sweetness is brought out by making the sap into syrup or sugar. The Potawatomie Indians used maple sap to make vinegar as well as sugar. Some sap was soured and used in the preparation of venison and dandelion greens.

Most methods for making syrup require long hours of cooking to reduce the sap to syrup. A method that is simple and just as effective is to concentrate the sap into syrup by freezing. We came across this method in *Mother Earth News* and immediately adopted it. First the tree must be tapped. If the tree is ready to be tapped, the inside of the hole will soon be moist and very soon sap will start trickling out. The tree could be tapped in more than one spot but more than two or three holes will overburden the tree. Tapping the tree requires no expensive equipment. To collect the flowing sap you will need tin cans or quart-sized plastic bags. You will also need some nails and a quarter-inch drill. With the drill, bore a hole, angled slightly upward, through the bark and insert a spile partway into the opening until half an inch of the spile remains on the outside. Plastic straws can be used for the spiles but hollowed-out sumac or elderberry stems work just as well. The spile should fit snugly into the hole. Nail a tin can or plastic bag underneath to catch the dripping sap. Every day for a week, empty the cans or plastic bags of their sap and put up fresh ones. In a week's time, every 4 trees should have yielded about 5 gallons of sap. Be sure to plug the holes up with wooden pegs when you are finished so that the tree is protected from invading insect pests and disease. Place the collected sap in empty milk cartons or other suitable containers and put the containers outside at night. The next morning, bring the frozen blocks inside and after about a third of the contents has melted, drain off the liquid and discard the ice. This freezing can be done in a deep freezer if the nights aren't cold enough. This first step reduces 5 gallons of sap to about 1½ gallons. Next freeze the concentrated sap and allow half of the ice to melt before separating the liquid and discarding the solid ice remaining. The second freeze should yield about 3 quarts of very clear and very sweet fluid. Finally, evaporate the concentrated sap on a kitchen stove until it is thick and syrupy. Be careful not to scorch it. The end result should be 1 pint of golden maple syrup for every initial 5 gallons of sap. To make sure you don't lose any of the sap during the freezing

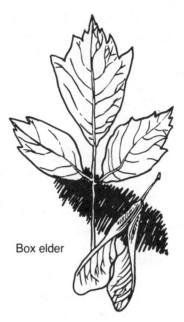

Box elder

process, you may want to melt the ice and put the maple-flavored liquid through both freezing processes again. In our opinion, this cold method is preferable to the energy-consuming boiling method.

Although the sugar maple is traditionally the tree tapped for making maple syrup, any maple will yield good syrup if it is a good-sized tree. Trees growing on southern slopes in sandy soil are usually the best. The other maples found in Indiana are the black sugar maple (*A. nigrum*), the red maple (*A. rubrum*), the silver maple (*A. saccharinum*), and the box elder (*A. negundo*). The black sugar maple is found throughout the state in the same habitat as sugar maples although it prefers a moister habitat. The trees are nearly identical, but the black sugar maple has darker bark and its leaves, which have broader, shorter lobes, are not as light on the underside. The black sugar maple is a hardwood maple and is often used for commercial production of maple syrup. The red maple is scattered infrequently throughout the state and is distinguished by its reddish twigs and red flowers. The silver maple is found in wet places such as swamps and low grounds scattered throughout the state. The five-lobed leaves are silvery beneath and the lobes more deeply cut than those of the sugar maple. The box elder is infrequent in the northern counties but increases in frequency in the southern counties and reaches its greatest size in the Southwestern Lowlands. It, like the silver maple, likes damp places and is found along streams, lakes, and swamps. The box elder does not have typical maple leaves. Instead, it has opposite, feather-compound leaves with three to five coarsely toothed leaflets; the end leaflet is often three-pointed. Other characteristics resemble the sugar maple. As stated earlier, any maple can be tapped and the quality of the sap depends more on the quality of the particular tree than on the type of maple.

If you would like to read a more detailed account on the art of sugaring, we recommend *The Maple Sugar Book* by Helen and Scott Nearing. This book has detailed directions on the boiling method for rendering sap into syrup. Besides learning about maple sugar, you will also get an insight into the Nearings' philosophy of life. As in their other book, *Living the Good Life*, the Nearings give their views on "how to live sanely and simply in a troubled world."

We are sure you won't have any trouble deciding what to do with your maple syrup but if you get your fill of French toast and pancakes, you should try Jann Jacobson's Maple Syrup Cheesecake. This is wonderfully easy to make and sinfully delicious. In a blender combine 1 pound softened cream cheese, 2 eggs, and ½ cup of maple syrup. Blend until smooth and pour into a cooled crust. Bake in a preheated 325° oven for 30–40 minutes until the center is firm. Chill and serve topped with whipped cream. Sliced fresh fruit or whole berries make an attractive and tasty garnish. A graham cracker or pastry crust is good with this but we prefer an oatmeal-sesame seed crust. Combine 1 cup dry rolled oats, ¼ cup whole wheat flour, ½ cup sesame seeds, 1 teaspoon cinnamon, and ½ to ¾ stick of butter melted with 1 tablespoon honey. Press into a 10-inch pie pan or square cake pan. Bake for 5–10 minutes in a 300° oven, if desired. The crust need not be baked before it is filled. If you do bake the crust first, let it cool completely before pouring in the cheesecake mixture. Then bake as directed.

If you feel like celebrating the joys of maple sugaring, the Parke County Maple Fair, held annually in Rockville, Indiana, features such activities as bus tours to sugar camps and a pancake-maple syrup meal.

Since the maple gives us not only maple syrup, but also beautiful fall foliage of bright yellow, orange, and scarlet, it is understandable that citizens of New York, West Virginia, Vermont, Wisconsin, and Canada have chosen the maple leaf to represent them.

The maple is tree-mendous.

New Jersey Tea

New Jersey tea (*Ceanothus americanus*) is a low shrub, one to three feet high, with somewhat branched stems, found in dry situations throughout Indiana. This member of the Buckthorn Family is especially frequent in the Lake Area and around the Dunes; in other parts of the state it is often found on the crests of black and white oak ridges. In the southern counties it is common on sandstone and limestone bluffs. This decorative plant has three-inch-long, alternate, oval leaves borne on short stems. The dark green leaves are pointed and finely blunt-toothed with pale undersides that are hairy and velvety to the touch. The leaves have three prominent ribs. The center rib runs to the pointed end and the other two ribs curve and nearly reach the end. The minute white flowers with dipper-shaped petals appear in June or July and form dense clusters at the end of long stems. In September and October, the fruit clusters appear. Each fruit is a three-celled capsule, with each cell containing one smooth light brown seed that is oblong and flattened on one side. The rootstalks are red and make a good red dye. The early pioneers frequently used the leaves as a tea substitute. This good-tasting tea contains no caffeine but has a rich, robust flavor. The leaves should be gathered while the flowers are in bloom (June–August). The tea may be made from fresh or dried leaves but dried are preferable. Dry the leaves by bundling them and hanging them in a dry room for several weeks. The tea is made by steeping 1 teaspoon of dried leaves in 1 cup of boiling water for 3–5 minutes until the desired strength is reached.

Despite its name, New Jersey tea is right at home in Indiana.

Wild Grapes

Six species of wild grape (*Vitis* sp.) are found in Indiana. They hybridize readily, so it is often hard to tell one from another. In general, grapes are woody vines with simple, alternate, heart-shaped, toothed leaves. The greenish yellow flowers have five petals. The round purple grapes are borne in clusters and taste a little tarter and have tougher skins than their domesticated counterparts. Most grapes favor moist soil and the riverbank grape *(V. riparia)*, found throughout the state in glaciated areas, is abundant in alluvial soil along streams. This grape is most frequent in the upper two-thirds of the state, especially north of the Wabash River. It is rare in hilly counties and absent from counties with no large streams. The riverbank grape has sharply toothed leaves with two short lateral lobes that are U-shaped at their base. In other respects it is similar to the frost grape *(V. vulpina)*, which is found along fences throughout Indiana and is most predominant in the central counties. Frost grape leaves have broad, convex teeth and no lateral lobes; the leaf base is V-shaped.

The fox grape *(V. labrusca)* is frequent in counties along the border of Lake Michigan, along the Kankakee River, and along the flats of the southeastern part of the state. Most cultivated varieties of grapes, including the Concord, are derived from the fox grape. The fox grape favors lime-deficient soil and is very abundant in Jennings and Ripley counties.

The summer grape *(V. aestivalis)* is scattered throughout the state but more frequent in the unglaciated uplands of the southern counties. The leaves are whitish or rusty underneath. The sweet winter grape *(V. cinerea)* is also a southern grape with its northernmost limit in Marshall County. The catbird grape *(V. palmata)* is found only on the low borders of sloughs and ponds in the lower Wabash Valley in Knox, Gibson, and Posey counties. The branchlets are bright red.

Although it is interesting to determine the species of grapes, it is not vital since all species are edible. The young tendrils can be eaten as a snack and the young leaves may be blanched 4 minutes in boiling water to use in stuffed grape leaves. We stuff 12–16 leaves with a mixture of 2 cups cooked brown rice, ½ cup chopped nuts, ½ cup sautéed mushrooms, ½ cup chopped green onions, and the juice of one lemon. Put some of the filling on each blanched leaf, roll, and put in a baking dish. Cover with white sauce and bake until heated through. Serve garnished with twists of lemon.

To can the grape leaves for later use, wash five-inch leaves, remove stems, and arrange in piles of ten. Roll each pile tightly and tie with string. Boil 2 quarts of water with ½ cup of salt. Add a few rolls at a time and cook until all the leaves have changed color (about 2 minutes after last addition of leaves). Remove the rolls from the water and pack into sterilized canning jars. Fill with boiling salted water and seal at once. Six dozen leaves can be packed into a quart jar.

Grapes are ripe in late summer or early fall and make excellent juice or jelly. To extract the juice, place the stemmed grapes in a large kettle and add just enough water to keep them from scorching. If you want spiced juice, add a few sticks of cinnamon and whole cloves. Bring the grapes to a boil, reduce heat and simmer for 10–15 minutes. Strain through a cheesecloth. Pour the strained juice into hot, sterilized jars and seal with double metal canning lids. Process for 20 minutes in a hot water bath.

Wild grapes have natural pectin so it is easy to make jelly from the juice. To increase the pectin content of your juice just include a few underripe grapes with the ripe ones. Take 4 cups juice and put over low heat. Add 3 cups of honey and stir until well mixed. Increase the heat and rapidly bring to a boil. Immediately add 6 ounces (1 bottle) liquid pectin and, stirring constantly, heat to a full, rolling boil. Boil for 1 minute, immediately remove from heat, pour into hot, sterilized jars, and seal with paraffin.

We have read reports that the Indians dried the grapes, ground them (seed and all), and used them to thicken soups.

A final note of warning: The poisonous, grapelike berries of the moonseed vine (*Menispermum canadense*) could be mistaken for grapes by a careless forager. Moonseed bears a round black drupe with a whitish wax on the surface. However, the distinguishing characteristics are the number of seeds, the leaf margins, and the way the vine climbs. A moonseed fruit has only one seed, which is grooved and crescent-shaped, but a grape always contains more than one seed. Moonseed leaves are lobed and untoothed whereas grape leaves are toothed. Grapes climb by their tendrils, which twine around supports. Moonseed has no tendrils; its main stem twines.

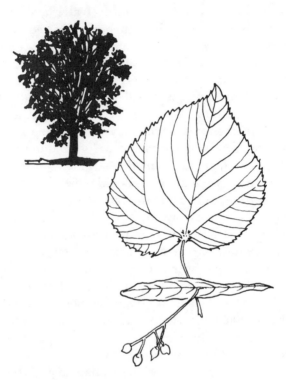

Basswoods

Basswood or American linden (*Tilia americana*) is a tall, stately tree found in rich, moist soils throughout the state. Basswood, which reaches its greatest development in Indiana, is usually found in the same woods with beech, maple, white ash, and red elm. In the southern counties basswood grows to great heights on the rocky bluffs of streams. The mature bark is deeply furrowed and dark gray brown. The large (five to ten inches), dark green, sharply toothed, alternate leaves are heart-shaped although they look somewhat lopsided at the base. The leaves are downy beneath. When the leaves are almost mature, fragrant white or yellow flowers, which have tufts of hair at the axils, appear. The flowers, which only bloom for three weeks in the spring, grow in flat-topped flower clusters with the central flowers unfolding first. Bees use these sweet flowers to make a light-colored, good-flavored honey. The woolly nutlike fruit, which is one-celled and a quarter-inch in diameter, is attached to a leafy bract. A sweet and fragrant tea can be made from the dried flowers. Spread out the flowers in a warm room until completely dried. Then steep 1 tablespoon of the dried flowers in 1 cup of boiling water for 5 minutes. We like our basswood tea sweetened with honey. This tea is not only delicious and refreshing but is also an aid to digestion.

In the Southeastern Till Plain, white basswood (*T. heterophylla*) can occasionally be found on the bluffs and slopes of ravines and streams. White basswood is identical to basswood except that the underside of the leaves is white. The tree is especially conspicuous when a breeze reveals these shimmering white surfaces. The fragrant flowers of white basswood are also used for tea.

Basswood jelly can be made from extra-strength basswood tea. The tea must be so strong that its color is almost brown. Mix together 3 cups mild-flavored honey and 1 cup tea. Heat to boiling very quickly and add ½ bottle (3 ounces) of liquid pectin all at once, stirring constantly. Heat to a full, rolling boil, boil 1 minute, then immediately remove from heat. Pour quickly into sterilized jelly glasses and seal with paraffin at once. This makes about five 6-ounce glasses of jelly. Basswood honey, if you can find it, would definitely intensify the flavor. If you have never had the good fortune to taste basswood honey, the jelly will give you an idea of how delicious it is.

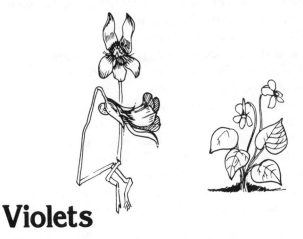

Violets

Violets (*Viola* sp.), the vivacious heralds of spring, are common in shady places throughout the state. Although the blue violet (*V. sororia*) is the most common, Indiana has twenty-four species of violets found in gardens, yards, along roadsides, and in other waste places. These delicate, slender perennials have several hairy, branching stems that rise from thick fleshy roots. The bright green leaves are oval or heart-shaped with coarse rounded teeth or smooth margins, depending on the species. The five-petaled flowers may be white, blue, or yellow and the fruit is a podlike capsule. Since violets hybridize freely, it is difficult to identify the species precisely, but all are edible.

The mucilaginous leaves and stems are rich in vitamin A and may be eaten raw in salads or added to soups or stews and, like okra, they are a thickening agent. Steaming the leaves and stems with lemon peel brings out their delicate flavor. The flowers are rich in vitamin C and we often eat them raw as a natural vitamin tablet or add them to salads. Violet tea is made by steeping a handful of blossoms in boiling water until the desired strength is reached.

A dessert that makes any meal special is violet pudding. To prepare, place 1½ cups of packed blossoms in a pan with a cover and add 2 cups of boiling water. Cover and steep until cool. In the meantime, mix together 5 teaspoons unflavored gelatin and ¼ cup cold water in a saucepan. Add ¾ cup honey, ¼ teaspoon salt, and ½ cup lemon juice. Combine the violet tea mixture with this and bring to a boil over medium heat, stirring constantly. Pour into individual molds and chill until firm. Unmold and serve with small plumes of whipped cream.

The following recipe for violet blossom jelly was given to Linda Brooks by Bonnie Hiatt of Star City. We are including the recipe exactly as Mrs. Hiatt wrote it down.

Choose a beautiful day because half the fun is in picking the flowers. Gather about 2 cups of violets—no stems; just snap off the heads and don't worry about the little green part that clings to the flower. It's o.k. Put the blossoms in a shallow bowl and look them over for any hitchhiking bugs. Let the blossoms sit in the shallow bowl about one-half hour to give the remaining bugs a chance to leave. Remember, they have had their chance. Now, rinse the violets in cold water and put them in a quart jar. Cover them with boiling water, put the lid on, and let them infuse for 24 hours. The next day, they'll look awful, like bits of wilted lettuce floating in blue rit dye. And it smells worse. Never fear—strain out the blossoms and to two cups of infusion add the juice of one lemon (see how the color comes back) plus one box of powdered pectin. Bring to a boil. Add 4 cups of sugar (or honey) and bring to a boil again. Boil hard for one minute, then pour into sterilized jelly jars and seal. You'll have a batch of the loveliest jelly in the world! Flavor? It's sweet and tastes like violets, of course! You won't, however, want to plaster it thickly on toast, but a dab on a cracker is delicious; nice with afternoon tea and terribly gourmet. It also makes an impressive gift. Friends and neighbors will love you and if you happen to be a grandmother, your grandchildren will say, "Wow, look what my grandmother made!"

Another beautiful day in your book of memories.

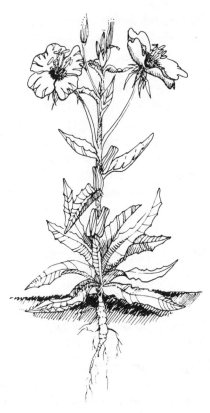

Evening Primrose

Evening primrose (*Oenothera biennis*) is a native biennial found in all kinds of habitats throughout the state. The first year, the plant grows a rosette of one- to six-inch-long, lance-shaped, stalkless leaves that lie flat on the ground. It stores food in its reddish starchy root and the second year sends up a stout reddish stem that is slightly hairy. The alternate leaves have prominent midribs and are dense giving the plant a full bushy look. At the top of the stem, clusters of pale yellow, four-petaled flowers, one to two inches wide, appear from June to September. (The stigma is X-shaped.) The short-lived flowers bloom only once, usually in the cool of the evening, and then close (under the hot sun). The erect seed pods are cylindrical with pointed tips. The peppery but edible root should be gathered in the early spring or late fall of the first year. The first-year rosette growth will usually be growing side by side with the stalked second-year growth thus making identification simple. The reddish root is the color of a beet but is shaped like a carrot. Since the root is peppery it should be cooked in 2 changes of water. The pepperiness of the roots is enhanced when they are served with a sweet and sour sauce.

To prepare the roots, boil 16–20 minutes in 2 changes of water until just tender. In the meantime slice four to six large mushrooms and chop four green onions (tops and all); sauté in a bit of oil until the onions are translucent. Add ¼ cup finely chopped celery and cook 1 minute longer. Combine ½ cup pineapple juice, ¼ cup honey, ¼ cup vinegar, 1 tablespoon soy sauce, and 2 tablespoons cornstarch. Add this to the skillet with the sautéed vegetables and cook over medium heat until thickened. Peel and thickly slice the cooked primrose roots and add to the skillet with 1 small green pepper cut into strips and one 8-ounce can of drained pineapple tidbits (juice pack). Cook 3–4 minutes until heated through and serve over brown rice.

The young leaves and shoots may be gathered in the spring and used sparingly in salads or cooked as greens in 2 changes of water. The leaves and shoots are peppery and are better used to enhance other foods rather than as a vegetable on their own. After boiling once, the leaves or shoots may be added to soup or stew and their mucilaginous quality will thicken it.

Persimmon

Visions of sugar plums may dance through your head as you pluck the rusty orange persimmon fruits, but if they are not ripe your visions will end in a pucker. The persimmon (*Diospyros virginiana*), a member of the Ebony Family, is native in Indiana from Franklin to Parke County. Thickets of this small or medium-sized tree adorn abandoned fields and roadsides. Although not native to northern Indiana, the persimmon has been introduced into yards there. However, the persimmon is most abundant in the unglaciated areas of southwestern Indiana. This slow-growing tree produces a large, pulpy berry, one- to one-and-a-half inches in diameter, that resembles a tiny jack-o'-lantern. The persimmon has the distinction of being the largest berry produced by any American forest tree. When fully ripe the fruit is sweet and delicious, but unripe it is harsh and puckery. Although the ripening time varies from tree to tree, a general rule of thumb is to pick them around the time of the first frost. (Contrary to popular belief, the frost does not ripen them.) The berries contain several large flat seeds and a pulp rich in iron, potassium, and vitamin C. The fruits are preceded by inconspicuous, yellowish white flowers that bloom in May.

The thick, four- to six-inch-long, alternate leaves are shiny and oval with sharp points and smooth margins. The deeply furrowed bark, which resembles alligator hide, breaks into hard, square blocks, dark gray to black, separated by furrows that are cinnamon red along the bottom.

Every year after the first frost, a kind lady in Fulton County gives us permission to gather the plump orange fruits from the tree in her yard. We spread our old gathering sheet under the tree and shake the branches gently. If the fruits are ripe, a gentle shake is enough to free them and they tumble onto our sheet. Those that cling to the branches are probably not ripe enough to eat. The quality of the fruit and the number of seeds will vary from tree to tree.

Once you find a suitable tree gather your fill and make puddings, breads, butter, or whatever your imagination brings you. There are as many persimmon pudding recipes as there are cooks. If you don't believe us, just visit the Persimmon Festival held every fall at Mitchell, Indiana, in Lawrence County for an orgy of persimmon eating. We have made several varieties of persimmon pudding but one that is traditional with us is Grandmother Bessie's Persimmon Pudding. Remove the flower caps and run the persimmons through a colander to make 3 cups of persimmon pulp. Combine the pulp with 2 beaten eggs, ¾ cup sour milk or yogurt, and ¼ cup melted butter. Add 2 cups unbleached white or whole wheat flour that has been mixed with 1 teaspoon soda, 1 teaspoon baking powder, and a dash of salt. Pour into a well-greased 8 x 8 x 2 inch square pan. Bake in a preheated 225° oven for 2 hours. Then prick the pudding all over with a toothpick and pour over it a gently heated mixture of ½ cup honey, ¼ cup water, and a lump of butter. Return the pudding to the oven for 10 more minutes and serve hot or cold with freshly whipped cream.

We also enjoy persimmon cobbler made by combining 3 cups pulp, ¼ cup honey, and ½ cup orange juice. Pour this mixture into a greased 2-quart casserole. In a separate bowl

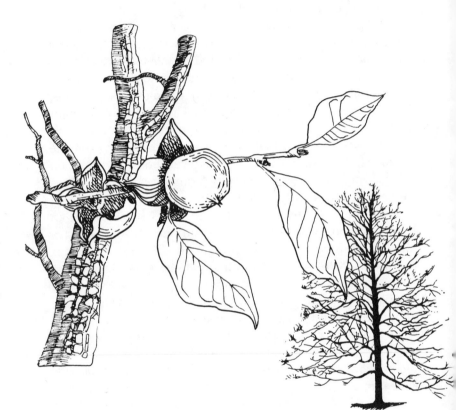

mix 1½ cups whole wheat flour, 1 cup cornmeal, 1½ tea-spoons soda, 1 teaspoon each of cinnamon and ginger, ½ teaspoon salt, and 1 tablespoon grated orange rind. To this mixture add a combination of ½ cup light molasses, ½ cup honey, 1 cup hot water, and 2 beaten eggs. Pour over the persimmon pulp and bake in a preheated 350 ° oven for 35–45 minutes. Cool 10 minutes and serve with cream.

Just when you think all the fresh fruits are gone, along come persimmons, just in time for Indian Summer Ice Cream. Soften 1½ teaspoons of gelatin in ¼ cup water. Thoroughly blend ¼ cup honey, 1½ cups light cream, 4 egg yolks, and a dash of salt. Cook this mixture in a double boiler until it is thick enough to coat a spoon. Stir in the gelatin and cook until dissolved. Cool and then add the grated rind of two lemons, 2 tablespoons lemon juice, 1 cup cream, and 2 cups persimmon purée. Mix well and freeze. This will make 1½–2 quarts.

A nice wintertime treat to have on hand is persimmon but-ter. For every 2 quarts of pulp combine ½ cup of honey, cin-namon and ginger to taste, 1 tablespoon each of grated orange and lemon peel, and 1 cup orange or lemon juice. Mix with pulp and cook until bubbling hot and thickened, then pour into hot, sterilized jars, and seal.

If you gather more persimmons than you can use right away, turn them into pulp, sweeten with honey, and cook until bubbling hot. Pour into hot, sterilized jars, seal, and process 30 minutes in a hot water bath. The canned pulp may be used in any recipe calling for fresh persimmon pulp.

The full-grown leaves may be gathered in summer, dried, and made into a tea that is rich in vitamin C.

Although the persimmon is usually a small or medium-sized tree, there is a giant persimmon growing near Johnson, Indiana, in Gibson County. This tree is 80 feet tall with a branch spread of 73½ feet and a trunk circumference of 13 feet. The American Forestry Association classifies this per-simmon as a champion tree.

We think that persimmons are champions regardless of their size. Others must have agreed: The Latin for persimmon, *diospyros*, means "fruit of Zeus." The common name, persimmon, is of Algonquian origin and is taken from the Delaware word *pasimenan*, which means "dried fruit."

Milkweed

Milkweed (*Asclepias syriaca*) is a sun-loving annual common in moist soil along roadsides and railroads, in cultivated and fallow fields, and in open woods throughout Indiana. It has a stout, unbranched central stalk, two to five feet tall, covered with downy hairs. The thick, stalkless leaves are two to four inches wide, four to nine inches long, and oblong or oval in shape with wide central ribs. The leaves occur in opposite pairs and are light green above with a lighter underside. All parts of the plant exude a sticky, thick, milky sap when broken. Fragrant globular clusters of numerous plump flowers appear in midsummer; these range in color from lavender pink to purple. Each tiny flower has five long petals that bend back around the stem, five hairy sepals, and five nectar horns. Any member of the milkweed genus can be recognized by these unique five-parted flowers. The large green pods, three to five inches long, which appear in late summer, are covered with wartlike bumps. At maturity they split, releasing silk-tufted seeds, which float through the air like miniature parachutes. If the pods are gathered just before they burst and the brown seeds removed, the silky strands may be dried and used to stuff pillows.

Young shoots under eight inches high may be gathered and prepared as an asparagus substitute although their flavor is much more pronounced than that of asparagus. When preparing any part of the milkweed, it is a good idea to cook it in 2 or 3 changes of water to remove the slightly bitter taste. The young sprouts may be located by finding last year's old, dry milkweed stalks. Rub the fine down off the shoots and plunge them into boiling water. Return to a boil and boil for 1 minute. Drain and repeat first step. On the third or last boiling, cook the shoots for 10 minutes or until tender. Serve with butter or cheese sauce. The young leaves are rich in vitamins A and C and they may be eaten as greens if prepared like the shoots. A good topping for the greens or shoots is a white sauce that has had ½ to 1 cup of sour cream added to it just before serving.

The young unopened flower buds may be gathered while still in tight clusters and eaten like broccoli. Cover the buds with boiling water and boil until tender, changing the water 2 or 3 times. Tomato sauce makes an excellent topping for these buds. While the buds are cooking, melt 2 tablespoons of butter in a heavy skillet and blend in 2 tablespoons of flour and ½ teaspoon of basil. Add 2 cups of tomato juice gradually and cook, stirring constantly, until the sauce is thick and smooth. Season with ¾ teaspoon garlic salt and ¼ teaspoon pepper. Pour the sauce over the hot, cooked buds and top with grated Parmesan cheese.

The young pods may be eaten like okra if gathered when they are no more than one inch long and before the silky seeds begin to mature. The pods will boil down to a soft, mucilaginous mass that is very tasty. Once again, 2 or 3 changes of boiling water are recommended to insure against bitterness. The pods and buds are an unappetizing grayish green before they are cooked but during cooking turn a beautiful bright green. The boiled pods are good served over croutons and topped with cheese sauce or tomato sauce—the softness of the cooked buds is complemented by the crispness of the croutons. Another way to prepare the pods is to blanch them in 2 changes of water, then slice into chunks, and roll them in cornmeal. Fry in butter and serve immediately.

The milky sap is reported to make a good chewing gum but we do not like it. The Miami Indians used the sap to rid themselves of warts. We have tried this with great success. Apply some of the sap every day until the wart is gone, usually two to three weeks. Historians have hypothesized that milkweed may have been cultivated by the Potawatomie Indians. Milkweed grew so close to the wigwams that it could have been planted there, since the Potawatomies used it for food and fiber.

Poisonous dogbane (*Apocynum*), which also exudes a milky secretion and occupies the same habitat as milkweed, might be confused with milkweed. However, there are at least three easy ways of telling the two plants apart. Dogbane, unlike milkweed, is not downy or hairy; instead, it is very smooth. Milkweed has one central stalk and does not branch; dogbane branches. Dogbane flowers, which are white or pink, sometimes with dark pink stripes inside, are shaped like tiny bells, and look nothing like milkweed flowers.

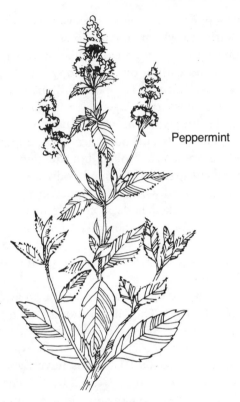

Peppermint

The Mint Family

Spearmint and peppermint are aromatic herbs readily identified by their distinct mint odor, expecially when the stems or leaves are crushed. Both plants have branched, square stems and sharply toothed opposite leaves. Spearmint (*Mentha spicata*) was cultivated by the pioneers for its medicinal qualities and is now a frequent escape found in wet places along roadsides, streams, and lakes throughout the state. The smooth purple or green stem is one to two feet tall when mature and has lance-shaped, stalkless leaves that are sharply pointed and have irregular teeth. The light purple flowers are borne in dense, pointed clusters at the end of a central stalk.

Peppermint (*M. piperita*) is another escape found throughout the state, especially in the northern part; it too prefers a moist habitat along fences, roadsides, streams, and lakes. Peppermint is one and a half to three feet high when mature and has a pronounced menthol flavor. The evenly toothed, downy leaves, narrower than those of spearmint, are borne on short stalks; the purple flowers form loose spikes that are not as tapered as those of spearmint. Since mints hybridize readily, it is nearly impossible for anyone but a trained botanist to tell various members of the family apart with any certainty. However, many species are easily identified by their square stems and mint aroma. All may be used in jellies, teas, or sauces, although the quality will vary from plant to plant.

Many frequently encountered plants belong to the Mint Family. Catnip (*Nepeta cataria*) is a familiar mint found throughout Indiana. Bergamot or bee balm (*Monarda fistulosa*) is a tall plant with bright purple flowers arranged in crownlike heads. Horehound (*Marrubium vulgare*), which has a downy white covering, is used to make horehound candy. Pennyroyal (*Hedeoma pulegioides*) is a small herb common in pastures and fields. Skullcap (*Scutellaria lateriflora*) and ground ivy (*Glecoma hederacea*) are popular as medicinal teas. Nearly all mints have been praised for their calmative qualities and their ability to cure nausea, but most people enjoy peppermint and spearmint teas and sauces because they taste so good. The leaves may be used fresh or dried. As a general rule, ⅓ to ½ teaspoon dried mint is equal to 1 tablespoon of fresh mint. The proportion depends on the age of the dried mint since the flavor of dried herbs deteriorates in storage. To make mint tea, steep 6 tablespoons fresh or 1 tablespoon dried mint leaves in a cup of boiling water until the desired strength is reached. Add honey or lemon juice and drink warm or serve over ice. This fragrant tea is rich in vitamins A and C and is said to be good for colds and headaches as well as upset stomachs. A large handful of mint leaves tossed into a hot bath is soothing to both body and soul.

To make mint sauce, combine ½ cup chopped fresh (or 4 teaspoons dried) mint leaves with ½ teaspoon salt, 1 teaspoon honey, ½ cup vinegar, and 2 tablespoons water. Marinate 1 hour before serving with lamb or vegetables.

We like to make mint dressing to put on crisp green salads. Combine ½ cup salad oil, ¼ cup tarragon vinegar, ½ cup finely chopped fresh mint, 1 teaspoon of salt, and ¼ teaspoon of freshly ground pepper. This is better if you let it stand 2 hours before using.

Mint jelly is as lovely to look at as it is to eat. It is also very easy to make. Pour ¾ cup of boiling water over 4 tablespoons of dried mint leaves, cover, and let stand for 20 minutes. Strain and add enough water to make ¾ cup. Add 2½ cups of mild honey and heat to boiling. Stir in 3 ounces (½ bottle) liquid pectin. Heat to a full rolling boil, remove from heat at once, and pour into sterilized jelly jars. This makes about 4 cups of jelly. This jelly does not have the garish green color of mint jelly that comes from the supermarket; it is a soft natural color that can only be described as a "golden green."

Elderberry

One New Year's Eve we welcomed the new year with a
bottle of homemade elderberry wine. What a wonderful way
to begin a year! American elder or elderberry (*Sambucus
canadensis*) is a showy, erect shrub, five to twelve feet high,
which forms thickets in wet open woods and along lakes,
streams, and fences throughout the state. The opposite compound leaves consist of five to eleven lance-shaped leaflets
that are arranged in pairs along a common axis. The leaflets
have pointed ends and are sharply toothed. In June and July,
tiny, white, five-pointed, star-shaped flowers are borne in
large flat clusters, called elder blow, which are approximately eight inches across. The flowers precede heavy clusters of small (usually less than a quarter inch in diameter)
purplish black berries, each of which contains three minute
nutlike seeds. Ripe elderberries can be found from July until
October.

This woody shrub only lives from three to five years but it
is a prolific root sprouter so thickets rarely die out. The berries are rich in vitamin C but lack acidity, so they are better
cooked than raw. When cooking always add lemon juice (or

sumac juice) to enhance the flavor. The elderberries may be
used to make excellent cobblers or pies. We especially like
elderberry-apple pie. Slightly crush 2 cups of elderberries
and combine with 1½ cups of apples, 3 tablespoons quick
tapioca, and ½ cup honey. Pour into an unbaked 9-inch pie
shell and top with a lattice of pastry strips. Bake in a 425°
oven for 10 minutes, then reduce the heat to 350°, and bake
for 20 minutes more. Topped with ice cream and served
while still warm, this pie is unbeatable.

Elderberry ice cream, anyone? Strange as it may sound, it
is actually quite good. Combine 1 pint of crushed elderber-

ries, 1 tablespoon lemon juice, and the grated rind of one lemon. Let this marinate while you prepare the ice cream mixture. Mix together 1¾ cups evaporated milk, ½ cup honey, and 1 teaspoon vanilla. Heat gently until warm. Add 2 teaspoons gelatin that has been softened in ½ cup water. Cool completely, add the elderberries and pour into a cake pan. Freeze this mixture in the freezer or freezing compartment of the refrigerator until it is thick but not stiff. (Watch closely; this takes only 15–25 minutes.) When thickened, whip thoroughly and fold in 1½ cups cream that has been whipped until it stands in soft peaks. Freeze at coldest setting until firm. This makes 1½–2 quarts.

Elderberries may be sun-dried between screens, then reconstituted in hot water to be eaten either stewed or added to muffins, biscuits, or pancakes. Juice extracted from the berries may be drunk plain or mixed half and half with apple or sumac juice. To store for the winter, heat the juice to a rolling boil and pour into hot, sterilized quart jars. Seal with double metal canning lids and process for 20 minutes in a hot water bath. This juice or juice mixture may also be used for jelly.

To make elderberry jelly, combine 3 cups of elderberry juice (or a mixture of elderberry and apple juice), 2 tablespoons lemon juice, and 1¾ ounces (one box) powdered pectin. Bring to a boil and immediately add 3 cups mild honey. Simmer 6 minutes, pour into hot, sterilized jelly jars, and seal with paraffin.

The berries or flowers may be used to make elderberry wine. Kin Hubbard, Brown County philosopher and creator of Abe Martin, said that "Elderberry wine makes a fine fall gargle." We have a friend whose father makes elderberry wine every year. To make elderberry wine, wash 4 pounds of stemmed elderberries and place them in a large bowl with ½ pound of chopped raisins. Pour a gallon of boiling water over the elderberries and raisins, stir well, and cover the bowl.

Leave the bowl for two weeks, then strain off the liquid into a pan, and discard the berries. Add 3 whole cloves to the liquid and bring to a boil. Pour the liquid over three pounds of sugar in a large bowl. Stir well. When the liquid is lukewarm, stir in ½ ounce of yeast, cover the bowl, and leave for three days. After three days the wine is ready to bottle. Strain, pour into bottles, and cork loosely. Keep a check on the corks so that they do not pop out. In about two or three weeks, add a little sugar to each bottle and recork. This wine is ready to drink in six months but it will improve with age.

The elder flowers may be steeped and drunk as a tea or added to pancake and muffin batter. We enjoy elderberry flower fritters; just follow the directions given for day lily fritters, p. 43.

This useful shrub has hollow twigs that may be used to make flutes, whistles, or maple syrup spiles. The fresh leaves are a good prevention against worms and insects when laid around young cucumbers, melons, or cabbages. If its edibility and usefulness aren't enough, the elderberry makes a lovely ornamental that graces your yard as well as feeds your family. Who could ask for more?

Jerusalem Artichoke

The Jerusalem artichoke (*Helianthus tuberosus*), some-times called earth apple or sunchoke, is a New World plant and one of our most common sunflowers. Indians made great use of the tubers and planted them around their villages; as a result, archaeologists are often able to locate the sites of Indian villages by the presence of large stands of Jerusalem artichokes. Spanish explorers learned of the plant from the Indians and carried it back to Europe where it was culti-vated in gardens. The English corrupted the Spanish word for sunflower, *girasol*, calling it Jerusalem. "Artichoke" pre-sumably comes from its taste, which is supposed to resemble the globe artichoke. However, earth apple is a more fitting name. The sweet, knobby tubers are nonstarchy and crisp and sweet like apples when eaten raw. They add a welcome crunch to all kinds of salads. They are good cubed and served with vinegar and oil dressing or hard-boiled eggs and mayonnaise. The artichokes make a good substitute for water chestnuts in Chinese recipes. Easily digested, they are delicious peeled and baked until tender or boiled 15–20 minutes. Serve them with butter, cream, or cheese sauce. Cooked, their texture is a bit watery but very flavorful.

To make Sunchoke Soup, boil 1 pound peeled, halved chokes with 4 stalks chopped celery in 2 quarts water for 15 minutes or until tender. While this is boiling, sauté 1 cup chopped onions, 1 cup sliced mushrooms, and 2 cloves garlic in a bit of oil until soft. Add the sautéed vegetables to the boiled vegetables; purée them in the blender until smooth. Return the purée mix to the stove; add 1 cup light cream and salt and pepper to taste. Heat just to boiling but do not allow to boil. Serve hot garnished with parsley.

This perennial is common in open moist areas along streams, ditches, and roadsides throughout Indiana. The Jerusalem artichoke is quite variable, but its tuberous roots make it readily identifiable. The stout stem has elongated-oval leaves that are hairy and rough. The leaves are alternate near the top of the plant but may be opposite below. Each leaf has a sharply tapering point and three prominent ribs on the underside. The golden yellow flower heads look like the familiar garden sunflower except that they are smaller. The Jerusalem artichoke is usually five to twelve feet high. The best time to harvest the tubers is in fall or early winter before the ground freezes but after the first frost, which seems to improve their flavor. They can also be dug in February or March as soon as the ground thaws. Once dug, the artichokes can be kept for two to three weeks in a cool, dark place.

Chicory

Chicory (*Cichorium intybus*) is a native of Eurasia that resembles dandelion when young. It is found in hard, dry clay or dry sandy soils along roadsides and in open places throughout the state. The lobed or spatula-shaped basal leaves are three to six inches long and thicker than dandelion leaves; they have toothed margins. These basal leaves form rosettes above a deep taproot. As the plant matures, it becomes hairy and branching with purplish leafstalks and midribs. The stalk oozes a milky sap when broken. The stem leaves are small and alternate. The branched stalks bear stalkless, ragged blue flowers. These delicate blue flowers have petals that are notched or toothed. The flowers usually close by early afternoon and do not open in bright, hot sunlight. The young leaves may be gathered and eaten as greens after boiling in one or two changes of water; they taste like dandelions. When using the leaves in salad, blanch them first. Blanched leaves may also be used to make Chicory Purses. These are little yeast rolls filled with savory chicory greens. To prepare, dissolve one package of yeast in 2 cups warm water. Add 1 tablespoon salt, ¾ cup melted butter, and 5 cups unbleached white or whole wheat flour. Knead in 1½ more cups of flour. Put in a bowl, cover, and place in a warm oven until doubled. Meanwhile, make the filling by combining 3 cups chopped, blanched chicory leaves, 3 minced onions, ½ cup pecans, ½ cup olive oil, juice of 3 lemons, and 1 tablespoon of salt. After the bread has doubled in bulk, punch down and knead. Roll the dough out to a ⅛-inch thickness and cut into 5-inch squares. Put some of the filling in each square and fold to make a triangle. Seal the edges by pinching them together, and place on a buttered cookie sheet. Brush with melted butter and bake in a preheated 450° oven for 25 minutes until well browned. The tantalizing aroma of baking bread will fill your house and whet appetites for these weed sandwiches.

The crown, which is the white underground part of the leaves and the top of the root, may be eaten exactly like dandelion crowns. The cooked crowns can be used to make a colorful confetti salad. Combine 1 cup cooked, quartered chicory crowns, 1 cup cooked green beans, 2 cups cooked kidney beans, 1 cup diced celery, 2 cups cooked brown rice, and ½ cup chopped green pepper. Marinate in a mixture of ½ cup oil, ½ cup wine vinegar, and 1 tablespoon honey until the salad is well chilled. Serve with rings of sliced red onion. This salad is a whole meal in itself.

Although the roots may be gathered anytime, summer is the best time to gather them to make into a coffeelike beverage. Peel off the outer layer of the roots, and roast them in a slow oven until they are dark brown and snap easily. Grind them and brew as you would coffee, or brew half and half with coffee. This chicory-coffee mixture is popular in the South, where it is sold in the supermarkets. Because chicory is stronger than coffee, if you are brewing chicory alone, use an amount one-third to one-half less than your normal measure of coffee. This chicory beverage is not good if reheated so drink your fill while it is hot.

Like dandelion roots, chicory roots may be brought in and forced in the basement for winter eating. The roots should be well watered. The leaves and crowns grown in the absence of light are mild and delicious.

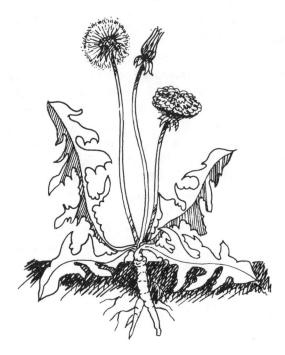

Dandelions

For many people, spring does not officially arrive until they have picked and eaten their first batch of wild dandelion greens. Depending on your point of view, the dandelion (*Taraxacum officinale*) is a troublesome weed or a delicious, free vegetable. Dandelions are persistent and common in lawns, orchards, and fields and along roadsides throughout the state except in the southwestern counties, where they are less frequent. The red seed dandelion (*T. laevigatum*) is well distributed in northern Indiana and is common in sandy soils throughout the state. Although it prefers sandy soil, the red seed dandelion is adaptive and often occurs in the same habitat as the dandelion. For the wild food hunter, these plants differ only in name since they are nearly identical and are used the same.

Dandelion leaves form rosettes close to the ground, sprouting from a deeply forked perennial taproot. The leaves are oblong, narrowing at their base, with irregular opposite lobes that have coarsely toothed margins. The flowers form in the protected area of the rosette and in the spring when conditions become favorable, the plant sends up the brilliant yellow flower heads on the end of hollow leafless stems that contain a milky juice. The fluffy flower heads are composed of numerous ray flowers that ripple in the wind. The sun-loving flowers close on cloudy and overcast days. The flower heads turn into silky balls that release fuzzy winged fruits that often fill the air on breezy summer days. Blowing dandelion fluff is a favorite pastime of children and a boon to the reproduction of the plant.

The leaves are rich in iron, potassium, calcium, and vitamins A and C. They may be eaten as a green or added to salads. They should be gathered early in the spring before they become bitter. Once the flower has formed, it is too late—you must boil all the flavor and nutrition out of the leaves to remove the bitterness. To prepare, plunge young leaves into rapidly boiling water, return to a boil, then discard the water, and boil in fresh water until tender. Serve with butter, sour cream, or cheese sauce. The Potawatomie Indians ate the cooked greens with maple sap vinegar.

If you are going to use the leaves for salad, it is best to blanch them first. Chill the blanched leaves and top them with your favorite salad dressing or try Jann's Green Goddess Dressing. In a blender, combine 1 cup mayonnaise, ¼ cup buttermilk, 3 garlic cloves, 2 tablespoons wine vinegar, 2 tablespoons honey, and 1 teaspoon each of dried basil, tarragon, celery seed, and chives. Blend until smooth and serve with a salad of blanched, chopped dandelion leaves, chopped hard-boiled eggs, and chopped tomatoes.

The blanched leaves are also good in Dandelion Casserole. To make this main dish, combine 2 cups cooked rice, 1 cup grated cheese, 4 beaten eggs, 1 teaspoon salt, and 2 cups of blanched, chopped dandelion leaves. Pour into an oiled casserole and top with 4 tablespoons of wheat germ that has been mixed with 1 tablespoon of oil. Bake in a preheated 350° oven for 35 minutes.

The flavor of the leaves will be very mild if they are shaded or covered while growing. So if you have a favorite patch, cover them lightly with burlap or paper and they will not be bitter. The leaf rosette may also be drawn up and tied together to keep the inner leaves white and sweet.

Dandelion crowns are gourmet eating when sliced into salads or briefly cooked. The crown is the top of the root and the white base of the leaves. Sliced crowns are reminiscent of artichoke hearts and are truly excellent when cooked 5 or 10 minutes, then chilled in a marinade of ¼ cup lemon juice and ½ cup safflower oil.

In April or early May before the flowers come out, you can find the just-developing flower heads nestled in the rosette of leaves. These fluffy balls are very good when cooked in boiling water for 2–3 minutes, drained, and served with butter. In May after the flower heads have emerged, they may be picked, sliced, and added to pancake batter. The flower heads may also be used to make dandelion wine. Pick 1 gallon of dandelion flower heads early in the day while they are fresh and open. Wash the blossoms, put them in a large crock, and cover with 1 gallon boiling water. To keep the winefly out, cover the crock with a double thickness of cheesecloth. Set aside for three days, stirring twice each day. After three days, squeeze out and discard the flower heads. Pour the liquid into a large kettle and add 3 oranges and 3 lemons, chopped fine. Add 1 ounce yeast, stir well, and boil for 30 minutes. Return to the crock, cover with cheesecloth, and let ferment for three weeks. Strain through nylon cloth or filter paper and put into bottles. Cork loosely until it has finished working, then push the corks down tightly. You can tell if the wine is still working by holding a clear glass bottle filled with wine to the light. If masses of tiny air bubbles are rising to the top, the wine is not yet ready to cork securely. Once the wine has stopped working, it may be drunk right away or allowed to age.

Dandelion roots gathered in the early spring yield a turniplike vegetable. Peel and cook in 2 changes of water until tender and serve the roots swimming in sour cream. The roots may also be used to make a tasty caffeine-free coffee substitute. The roots may be gathered anytime but early spring is best. Scrub the roots, then roast them in a slow oven for 3–5 hours until they are dry and dark. (They should snap easily when broken.) Grind and prepare as you would coffee. This beverage is good on its own or can be brewed half and half with coffee.

The dandelion came over on the Mayflower and was considered a choice vegetable by our forefathers. However, somewhere along the line the status of dandelion changed from vegetable to weed. It is unfortunate that most people spend so much time trying to eradicate the dandelion instead of propagating it as a worthwhile vegetable.

In early spring when the first wild greens appear, we are always reminded of Hoosier poet James Buchanan Elmore and his poem "When Katie Gathers Greens." In this poem Jim Buck tells of his own love for wild greens and explains why his "heart leaps up with joy and hope / When Katie gathers greens." There is a feeling of renewal and joy when the snow melts at last and dock, dandelion, mustard, and poke sleepily emerge from their winter bed to welcome "the happiest day of spring."

If you do not want to wait until spring to enjoy your dandelion greens, the dandelion roots may be brought inside to the basement and forced for winter eating. Wait until after

the first hard freeze, then put the roots in a box in the basement and barely cover the root crowns with soil. Keep in the
dark and water well. In a short time, light yellow leaves will
appear. These are delicately flavored and wonderful for
salads or cooked as a green vegetable. Each root will produce several crops of leaves. Poke roots can be forced in the
same manner if you would like to prolong your enjoyment of
the tasty poke sprouts.

Destroying angel

Mushrooms:
Comments and Cautions

There is an abundance of mushrooms in Indiana but we have chosen to include only four—morels, shaggymanes, sulphur shelf mushrooms, and puffballs. These foolproof four are quite common and very easy to identify, and we think they taste much better than the cultivated mushroom (*Agaricus bisporus*) sold in the stores.

If you look for mushrooms other than the four listed, it is absolutely essential to have at least one good mushroom book with you. There is no way of telling whether a mushroom is edible just by looking at it or tasting it. Some of the worst-looking mushrooms are edible; some of the most deadly are both beautiful and delicious. As with all plants, when in doubt, don't eat it.

The most dangerous mushrooms belong to the group *Amanita*. These large, showy mushrooms are responsible for more deaths every year than all other mushrooms combined. Many members of this family have a faint to strong chlorine odor. However, the destroying angel (*Amanita verna*) is odorless. It is a ghostly white figure on the forest floor. Cap, stalk, and gills are firm and white. There is a ring or veil around the stalk. Amanitas also have a cup around the bottom of the stem. You may have to dig around the stem to find this bulbous base. It is a good rule to avoid any mushroom with a bulb or cup at the base of the stem. Amanitas come in different colors. *Amanita muscaria,* for instance, which has a cap covered with wartlike bumps, may be red, yellow, or orange. Do not even taste a mushroom you suspect of being an Amanita: Even a very small amount can be fatal. Unfortunately, the symptoms of Amanita poisoning may not appear until many hours after the mushroom is eaten—by then little or nothing can be done to help the victim.

Be certain you have identified a species carefully and that it is edible before you taste it. If you are trying a mushroom

Fly agaric (*A. muscaria*)

species for the first time, eat sparingly; a few people may have allergic reactions to species considered edible and choice. A few mushrooms that are nonpoisonous may become poisonous if alcoholic beverages are consumed within an hour or two after they have been eaten. Both morels and shaggymanes have been involved in cases of such poisoning. To be safe, do not drink alcoholic beverages for several hours after eating wild mushrooms.

Mushrooms are unobtrusive, often nestled in dead leaves or nearly hidden by rotting logs. Patience and a sharp eye are essential equipment for the mushroom hunter.

Morels

The morels (*Morchella* sp.), often called sponge mushrooms, are the most widely known and most sought-after
mushrooms in Indiana. The morel is generally two to six inches high with a broad stalk and an enlarged brown head.
The entire brown head or cap is ridged and pitted and looks
like a sponge. Both the cap and the pale stalk are hollow.
Morels fruit only in the spring and any morel-like mushrooms found in the summer or fall are probably false
morels (certain species of *Helvella* and *Gyromitra*). However,
a few species of false morels fruit in the spring along with
the true morels. (Although false morels are not poisonous to
everyone, they have been known to cause serious illness or
death to some people. Eat no more than half a mushroom
until you are sure of your own individual tolerance.) False
morels can be easily distinguished from true morels by their

caps, which are wrinkled rather than pitted and resemble the convolutions of a brain.

The best places to find morels are oak ridges, tulip-poplar stands with mayapples growing beneath them, and old apple orchards; they also favor burned-over bottomlands, drifts of decaying leaves, and the ground around elm stumps. Morels appear in the spring from mid-April through May after lots of rainfall. Their season is usually about three to four weeks long. Like all mushrooms, morels are best when collected in the early morning while they are still fresh and free from insects. Remember to avoid drinking any alcoholic beverages for about two hours after eating morels.

To prepare the morels for eating, place in a strainer and run cold water over them for about 3 minutes. Put the morels on a dish towel to dry. Do not soak them. Our favorite way to prepare these mushrooms is to fry the cleaned and halved morels lightly in butter. They may be sautéed au naturel or first dipped in beaten egg and cracker crumbs or flour then fried to a golden brown.

Since morels are hollow, they readily adapt themselves to stuffing. Steam 2 dozen cleaned mushrooms for 3 minutes, cut nearly in half lengthwise, and stuff with a mixture of 1 cup cooked rice or bulgur wheat, 1 teaspoon finely minced green onion tops, and ⅓ cup toasted sunflower seeds. Insert a cube of cheddar or Monterey jack in each mushroom, place in a casserole, and sprinkle on ¼ cup of melted butter. Cover and bake in a preheated 350° oven for 15–20 minutes.

Although the morels are delicious fresh, they may also be dried or frozen for future use. To prepare morels for freezing, sauté the cleaned mushrooms in butter, place in airtight plastic containers or plastic bags, then freeze. They should keep for several months. To dry, just spread the cleaned morels on screens and place in full sun where they will get good air circulation. The morels should be reconstituted in warm water before using and are best in soups or stews.

Shaggymane

The shaggymane (*Coprinus comatus*), usually four to six inches tall, has a cylindrical or bellshaped cap that is white with brownish shaggy scales. It is easy to recognize; no other mushroom looks quite like it. Another identifying characteristic is that the gills of young shaggymanes are white but they turn into an inky liquid as they ripen. This dissolution takes place within a few hours and once it has begun, not even refrigeration will stop it. For this reason, shaggymanes must be eaten within a few hours after you have picked them or nothing will be left but a wet, black mess.

Shaggymanes are found in groups on lawns, in grassy parks, and in both town and country in spring and fall. These mushrooms are quite watery when cooked and for this reason are nice in sauces that use their black juice. They are excellent in scrambled eggs although the telltale gray of the juice streaked through the eggs may put you off a little at first. Sauté 1 cup of sliced shaggymanes in butter until browned. Beat 6 eggs with ¼ cup heavy cream, salt and pepper to taste, and 1 teaspoon tamari sauce. Stir in 3 tablespoons freshly grated Parmesan cheese and 1 tablespoon finely minced green onion tops. Pour the egg mixture over the mushrooms and scramble lightly. Serve on toast or hot biscuits.

The delicate flavor of shaggymanes is greatly enhanced when they are baked in cream. In a buttered casserole, arrange 12 shaggymanes. Dot with bits of butter, salt and pepper to taste, and pour ½ cup cream over the mushrooms. Cover and bake in a preheated 400° oven for 15 minutes or until the shaggymanes are tender. Serve on hot, buttered English muffins or toast.

Baked shaggymane casserole is prepared by simply placing a triple layer of shaggymanes in a casserole, covering them with white sauce or cheese sauce, and topping with wheat germ. To make white sauce, melt 2 tablespoons of butter in a saucepan over low heat. Add 3 tablespoons flour and mix well. Cook for 2 minutes, then slowly add 2 cups milk, stirring constantly. Allow the sauce to thicken and stir occasionally to keep it from scorching. If cheese sauce is preferred, just add ½ cup shredded cheese (such as cheddar, Swiss, or Gruyère) after the sauce has thickened. Bake in a preheated 350° oven for 15 minutes or until the mushrooms are tender.

Sulphur shelf
and puffballs

Sulphur Shelf

The sulphur shelf (*Polyporus sulphureus*) is common throughout the state on old rotting logs and stumps and on standing trees, both living and dead. These mushrooms prefer oaks but are found on many other trees as well. Shelf mushrooms are found in late summer and early fall and their sulphur yellow, hairless caps overlap to form conspicuous rosettes on fallen logs. On standing trees, they grow as a series of shelves, one above the other. The fresh shelves sometimes have alternating bands of yellow and bright orange. Shelf mushrooms appear in the same place year after year.

If gathered while still young, the entire sulphur shelf is soft enough to eat but as it matures, only the outer inch or so is tender enough to use. Mature sulphur shelves are woody and totally inedible. The tender, young shelves when sliced, breaded, and fried in oil have a flavor like breast of chicken and are sometimes referred to as the "chicken of the woods." You can make mushroom burgers from shelf mushrooms (or puffballs) by slicing the mushrooms into thin strips and sautéing in oil until tender. Push the strips together to form a sandwich-size heap and add a slice of cheese. Cover skillet until cheese melts, then put mushrooms and cheese on a whole wheat bun. Top with tomato, lettuce, alfalfa sprouts, and mayonnaise. This is a gourmet treat.

Shelf mushrooms can be used to make a hearty mushroom barley soup. Dice 1 large onion and enough shelf mushrooms to equal 3 cups. Sauté in ¼ cup of butter until browned. Add 6 cups water and ¼ to ½ cup of tamari sauce. Bring to a boil; then add ½ cup pearl barley. Reduce heat, cover and simmer for 1 hour or until barley is tender. According to folklore, mushroom barley soup will make you wise. We can't promise wisdom but we can promise a flavorful soup.

Extra shelf mushrooms, like morels and puffballs, can be sliced, sautéed, and then packed into plastic freezer containers and frozen. This way you can enjoy nature's bounty all year long.

Puffballs

Puffballs (*Calvatia* sp.) are found throughout Indiana growing on the ground or on rotten wood. Puffballs are white and nearly round, and they vary in size from very small to as large as basketballs. Split vertically, puffballs have an interior that is uniformly smooth and white. If there are signs of a gill and stem structure, you do not have a puffball but rather an immature mushroom or button of the deadly Amanita. Always check for this before you eat any puffball. Puffballs growing on logs are usually pear-shaped but otherwise typical.

In ages past, puffballs were said to be snuffboxes of the devil because of the spore clouds that issue from the mature mushrooms when they are pressed between the thumb and finger. Once the spores have formed, puffballs turn yellowish then brown and become dry and powdery inside. Eventually they crack open to release the spores. Puffballs can be found all through the growing season but are most abundant in the fall.

Gather only those puffballs that are young and still firm and white inside. Peel and slice vertically. They may be diced and added to salads or cut into large slices, breaded with egg and flour, and fried in butter. Eat the slices as they are or layer the breaded and fried mushrooms in a casserole with slices of mozzarella cheese. Top with tomato sauce that has been simmered with sautéed onions and garlic. Sprinkle with Parmesan cheese, basil, oregano, and salt. Bake in a preheated 350° oven for 20 minutes; then enjoy your Puffball Parmigiana.

Puffballs are excellent raw and are delicious if cubed and marinated in oil and lemon juice. Combine ½ teaspoon dried oregano, salt and pepper to taste, 3 tablespoons fresh lemon juice, and ½ cup olive oil. Add 3 cups diced puffballs and mix thoroughly. Marinate at room temperature for at least 2 hours, then serve on a bed of shredded romaine lettuce. Puffballs are also good cut into sticks and French fried.

Edible but . . .

Indiana has a great wealth of wild edible plants, but many of them are not as appealing as others. We have tried to include only those plants that are the most desirable, the easiest to identify, and the most accessible. However, there are many other edible plants that could be eaten in an emergency, as a nibble, or just out of curiosity. Some plants we have deleted because they are rare or closely resemble a poisonous plant. Our intention here is to present a few of these "edible but . . ." plants so that the forager is at least aware of their existence.

The inner bark of the willows (Salicaceae), the poplar (*Populus*), the alder (*Alnus*), and the slippery elm (*Ulmus fulva*) can be eaten but don't really taste very good. The honey locust (*Gleditsia triacanthos*), a thorny tree found infrequently throughout the state, has long twisting pods with an edible pulp surrounding the hard seeds. Black locust (*Robinia pseudo acacia*) is a thornless tree which was a pioneer ornamental and is now a common escape. Although other parts of the tree are poisonous, the fragrant flowers are edible and make good fritters. Redbud flowers (*Cercis*

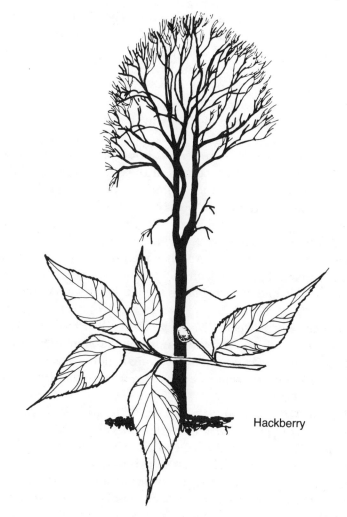

Hackberry

canadensis) are a pleasant addition to spring salads. The hackberry (*Celtis occidentalis* var. *canina*), a tree with elmlike leaves found in every county of the state, bears very small, dark purple to black drupes with large seeds and a thin, sweet pulp that tastes like dates. The pulp is so sparse that there is not enough for more than a nibble. The drupes are not ready to eat until after heavy fall frosts. The Indians used hackberries in pemmican, grinding up the drupes, seed and all. A similar nibble is the orange red drupes of the sugarberry (*Celtis mississippiensis*), a shrubby crooked tree confined to streams and lowlands in the Lower Wabash Valley.

The black haw (*Viburnum prunifolia*), found in moist woods, is native to every county of the state except the hilly counties where the southern black haw (*V. rufidulum*) is found. These berries are nearly all seed but the small amount of pulp that clings to the seed is very sweet. As James Whitcomb Riley said, "What is sweeter after all, than black haws in early fall?" Another member of the viburnum genus is nannyberry (*V. lentago*), frequent in the Lake Area, but we don't find the dry, large-seeded berries very appealing.

The American beech (*Fagus grandifolia*) is found in rich woods and ravines in every county of the state except the prairie counties. In autumn very small nuts mature; these can be roasted and eaten but the raw nuts should not be eaten in quantity.

The hop-tree (*Ptelea trifoliata*) is a small tree or shrub found infrequently throughout the state along the banks of streams. The round, flat fruit can be substituted for hops in beer making or used as a yeast to raise breads.

Berries of all sorts were once abundant throughout Indiana but due to drainage and cultivation many are now rare. Blueberries (*Vaccinium* sp.) and cranberries (*Vaccinium macrocarpon*) were once common in bogs in the Lake Area and black huckleberries (*Gaylussacia baccata*) were found in the wooded areas. Although deerberries were once common in the unglaciated area of the South-Central Oak and Mixed Woods, they now constitute more of a nibble when they can occasionally be found. Wild gooseberries (*Ribes* sp.) are infrequent throughout the state; they resemble domestic gooseberries except that the berries are covered with prickly spines that make them very difficult to eat. The currant (*Ribes americanum*) can sometimes be found but the small black fruit has an unpleasant odor unless well cooked. Chokeberries (*Aronia* sp.) are just what their name implies unless cooked into a jelly. The purple black berries are ripe in September and October and the plant can occasionally be found in wet soil. The partridge berry (*Mitchella repens*) is a creeper that prefers slightly acid soils. The red berries can sometimes be found in low, flat sweet gum and beech woods, on the crests and slopes of sandstone ridges, and in the black sand of black and pin oak woods of the northern part of the state.

The Indians ate many plants that are very hard to obtain unless you dive under water or wade into deep mud. Members of the Water Lily Family (Nymphaeceae) such as yellow pond lily (*Nuphar advena*) and the magnolia waterlily (*Nymphaea tuberosa*) are all very beautiful plants that are most frequent in lakes and sloughs in the Lake Area and have edible seeds and tubers. The American lotus (*Nelumbo pentapetala*), a magnificent plant with large pale yellow flowers, also has edible seeds and tubers but, although it was once common in deep ponds and shallow lakes, it is now nearly extinct. Watershield (*Brasenia schreberi*), a member of the same family, is frequent in three to five feet of water along the borders of lakes and in a few dredged ditches in the Lake Area although it is rare south of there. The young leaves are used as a potherb.

Some plants are edible only after they have been dried or boiled to neutralize the dangerous toxins they contain. An example is the marsh marigold (*Caltha palustris*), found in fresh, moving water such as lakes, streams, and ditches. It occurs most often in the Lake Area although it is sometimes

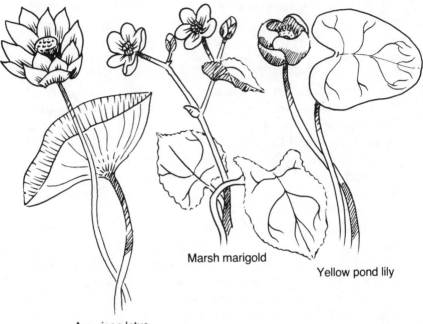

Marsh marigold

Yellow pond lily

American lotus

seen south of there. The yellow buttercuplike flowers make it
a conspicuous plant. The large, round, alternate leaves may
be gathered before the plant flowers and cooked as a
potherb; however, they contain the poison helleborin, which
is destroyed only by very thorough cooking for several hours,
and even then leaves an unpleasant taste. Water or mud
plantain (*Alisma* sp.) is scattered throughout the state in
ditches and wet places. The roots may be gathered from autumn to spring and eaten as a starchy vegetable after they
have been thoroughly dried, but they have a fiery taste that
may remain even after thorough drying.

Members of the Parsley Family (Umbelliferae) contain
some desirable wild edible plants, but this same family con-

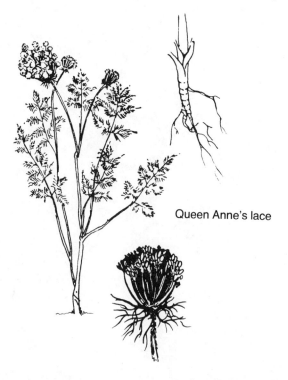

Queen Anne's lace

tains two plants that are deadly poisonous. It is difficult for the novice wild food forager to differentiate between members of this family; therefore, we do not recommend eating any of them. Wild carrot or Queen Anne's lace (*Daucus carota*), wild parsnip (*Pastinaca sativa*), cow parsnip (*Heracleum maximum*), purple stem angelica (*Angelica atropurpurea*), wild chervil (*Cryptotaenia canadensis*), sweet anise (*Osmorrhiza longistylis*), and sweet cicely (*O. claytonia*) are all edible members of the Parsley Family but because of their close similarity to the deadly poisonous poison hemlock (*Conium maculatum*) and water hemlock (*Cicuta maculata*), it is not advisable to use these wild plants unless you are *absolutely positive* of their identification. The novice

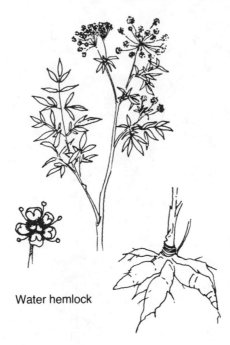

Water hemlock

forager can seldom be this sure. Poison hemlock is a native of Europe and is the hemlock responsible for the death of Socrates. The foliage as well as the roots is poisonous.

Ground cherry or husk-tomato (*Physalis* sp.) is a member of the Nightshade Family frequent in cultivated ground such as cornfields, clover fields, and pastures. This sprawling plant is also common in waste places and along railroads. The crushed stalks smell like tomato plants. Husk-tomato is easily recognized by the five-sided husk, which contains the yellow green pea-sized fruit. This straw-colored husk resembles that of its cultivated brother, the Chinese lantern plant, which is popular in dried flower arrangements. The fruits ripen late and will continue ripening in their husks even if they fall off the plant. The fruit should be eaten only after it

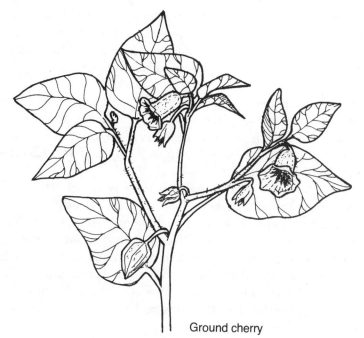

Ground cherry

turns orange yellow and is completely ripe. The fruits may be eaten raw or cooked into jam or pies.

Indian cucumber (*Medeola virginiana*) has sweet edible roots but it is rare, being found only infrequently throughout the state. In the hilly counties it prefers deep wooded ravines and in the northern part of the state is usually found in beech woods, in acid sandy flats, and on the lower slopes about lakes and swamps.

Lilies (*Lilium*), spiderwort (*Tradescantia*), merrybells (*Uvularia*), trillium (*Trillium*), and orchids (Orchidaceae) are all beautiful wildflowers that have some edible parts but we discourage eating them because of their rarity. In some counties in Indiana it is illegal to gather many of these flowers, especially trilliums and orchids.

Groundnut or potato bean (*Apios americana*) is also rare but can sometimes be found from late summer to spring in rich soils. The chains of tubers were favorites of the Indians and can be roasted or sliced and fried like potatoes.

The wild potato vine (*Ipomoea pandurata*), which is frequent throughout the state in moist soil along streams, resembles a morning glory and does, in fact, belong to the same family. This trailing vine has large roots resembling potatoes, which are buried deep in the ground and are often very hard to dig up.

Wild bean (*Phaseolus polystachios*) is a delicate, twining perennial occasionally found in dry woods scattered throughout some of the southern counties. The leaves have velvety undersides and the drooping pods contain four or five blackish beans that look like miniature kidney beans. In late summer or fall the beans can be gathered and used as you would dried garden beans. However, the beans are often hard to gather because the pods curl up and eject the seeds as soon as they are ripe.

Hog-peanut (*Amphicarpa bracteata*) is frequent in moist woods throughout the state. The twining stems are slender and bear three leaves, which resemble those of beans. The flowers look like pea flowers. The edible part is the underground fruits, which are like shelled beans although they are not as tender.

Wild lettuce (*Lactuca* sp.) unlike wild asparagus, is not as good as its cultivated counterpart. Wild lettuce is scattered throughout the state and has leaves that are good if gathered very young. We have never had any luck getting the prickly leaves early enough—we have always found them tough and bitter.

The young stems of thistles (*Cirsium* sp.) are edible but the prickly thistles must be removed carefully with scissors.

Mallows (*Malva neglecta*), also called cheeses, are frequent near dwellings throughout the state. The dark green round

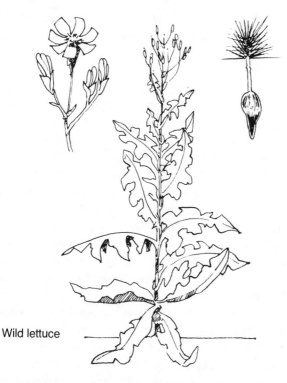

Wild lettuce

leaves, which are borne on long stems, may be eaten as a potherb but are not very flavorful. The flat, round seed capsules may be eaten as a nibble.

Virginia waterleaf or Shawnee salad (*Hydrophyllum virginianum* and *H. canadense*) is found infrequently in moist soil in all parts of the state except the southwest. It was a favorite food of the Indians. The leaves and top stems may be eaten raw; they also make a passable cooked green although the flavor is bland. The plant should be gathered and eaten while young since it becomes bitter with age.

Quickweed (*Galinsoga ciliata*) has succulent leaves that may be eaten as greens; it is found in cultivated fields, especially along the Ohio River.

Fireweed (*Erechtites hieracifolia*), found in marshes and burned-over areas throughout the state, has young tops and tender leaves that are edible in salads or as greens, if you do not mind their odor.

Cleavers (*Galium aparine*) belong to the same family as coffee and bear seeds that may be dried and roasted to use as a coffee substitute.

Woundwort (*Stachys hyssopifolia*), a square-stemmed, odorless member of the Mint Family, has crisp white edible tubers; it is found only in the northwestern counties. Goatsbeard or vegetable oyster (*Tragopogon*) is also found only in the north and northwestern counties. As the name implies, this plant has roots that taste like oysters when sliced, dipped in egg, floured, and fried. Goatsbeard has grasslike leaves and tall yellow ray flowers; it looks like a giant dandelion. It develops large seed heads similar to the smaller ones of dandelion.

Common burdock (*Arctium minus*) is common in rich soil about homes throughout the state. It is easily recognized by its large rhubarblike leaves and many burrs. In Japan a variety is grown as a garden vegetable. Very young burdock leaves and stems may be eaten after boiling in two changes of water; their flavor is similar to vegetable oyster. The root can be eaten and is good-tasting, but we find the Indiana variety a little tough.

If you have an urge for chewing gum and are removed from commercial sources, try chewing some sap from the sweet gum tree (*Liquidambar styraciflua*). The sweet or red gum is found in low woods in the southern half of the state and is usually abundant when it does occur.

Plantain (*Plantago* sp.) is a common weed in yards and waste places throughout Indiana. Although the greens are edible, they are usually stringy and not very tender.

Japanese knotweed (*Polygonum cuspidatum*) is an immigrant from Japan that spreads rapidly, forming thickets; it is

Plantain

found throughout the state. This sun loving plant, four to eight feet tall, has jointed hollow stems and alternate oval leaves. The peeled young stems may be cooked quickly and have a tart taste like rhubarb. The young shoots resemble asparagus and may be prepared in the same way.

Sweet fern (*Comptonia peregrina*) is not really a fern but rather a shrub with fernlike leaves. Sweet fern is scattered throughout the northwestern counties in acid soil and in black, sandy soil in open places in pin oak woods. It forms large colonies and is usually found alongside bracken fern. Tea made from sweet fern leaves has been described as fragrant and delicious but we find the flavor medicinal.

The Ginseng Family (Araliaceae) contains the well-known ginseng (*Panax quinquefolium*) and dwarf ginseng (*P. trifolium*). Although once abundant in Indiana, these two ginsengs are now rare due to intense foraging for their roots, which were used medicinally in China and brought high

Ginseng

prices. At one time large amounts of ginseng were exported
to China, where it has long been valued for its restorative
qualities. The Chinese and Koreans believe that the root
maintains health, prolongs life, and insures virility. The
early ginseng boom at the turn of the century exhausted
Hoosier supplies, but since then it may have staged a come-
back. Ginseng is a slow-growing plant—it takes from five to
eight years to produce a medicinally usable root. Young, un-
dersized roots do not dry well; they become hard and brittle.
The fleshy mature root is two to four inches long and usually
forked with two or three roots above the fork. With a little

imagination you could say it was shaped like a man. The root has prominent circular wrinkles on it. It should be dug up rather than pulled or it will break. Ginseng has a whorl of three fan-compound, five-parted leaves and greenish yellow flower clusters that mature into bright crimsom berries. In the fall, ginseng foliage turns golden yellow, making the plant very conspicuous on the forest floor. Ginseng favors soil formed from the acid leaf mold of hardwoods and it is usually found in deep shade in ravines or on the gentle north slopes of hardwood forests such as oak or sugar maple. We found ginseng growing along the bluffs of Sugar Creek. For use as a medicine the roots are gathered in the fall, scrubbed clean with hot water and a stiff brush, and dried in a well-ventilated room. Pieces of the dried root are eaten daily to restore vigor and prolong life. Ginseng root could be eaten raw as a nibble and the leaves may be used to make tea. If you would like to read an interesting and romantic account of the life of a Hoosier ginseng and herb gatherer, read *The Harvester* by Gene Stratton Porter, a Hoosier writer and naturalist.

Wild sarsaparilla (*Aralia nudicaulis*), also a member of the Ginseng Family, is found in the northern counties and occasionally in the west central counties. Its long roots are used in making root beer. The long plump roots of spikenard (*A. racemosa*) are also used in root beer or cooked as a vegetable. Spikenard occurs in rich woods throughout the state.

Hercules-club (*A. spinosa*) is a shrub or small tree covered with spines. It is found in the south-central counties and the southeastern counties as well as in people's yards. The young expanding leaves, which resemble fiddlehead ferns, may be eaten as a potherb if gathered young enough, that is, before the prickles on the leafstalks harden.

Although there are other "edible but ..." plants in Indiana, we have tried to include the most significant. For the modern forager wild foods will probably not be a replacement for cultivated foods, but, rather, a supplement to alleviate the monotony of our civilized diets. We also believe that eating from the wild helps put us back into the ecology of nature. The Indians' way of life was closely related to plant ecology but civilization has brought about a drastic change in our relationship with wild nature. The experience of gathering and eating wild foods helps bring us back into communion with nature and we are fortunate that Indiana offers so many wild foods to choose from. We hope that you will discover, as we have, that Indiana is a paradise of wild fruits and vegetables.

HELPFUL BOOKS

Angier, Bradford. *Feasting Free on Wild Edibles.* Harrisburg, Pa.: Stackpole Books, 1972.

Anson, Bert. *The Miami Indians.* Norman, Okla.: University of Oklahoma Press, 1970.

Christensen, Clyde M. *Edible Wild Mushrooms.* Lafayette: Cooperative Extension Service, Purdue University.

Cobb, Boughton. *A Field Guide to the Ferns.* Boston: Houghton Mifflin Co., 1963.

Deam, Charles C. *Flora of Indiana.* Indianapolis: Indiana Dept. of Conservation, Division of Forestry, 1940.

Deam, Charles C. *Shrubs of Indiana.* Indianapolis: Indiana Dept. of Conservation, 1932.

Deam, Charles C. *Trees of Indiana.* Indianapolis: Indiana Dept. of Conservation, 1918.

Durand, Herbert. *Field Book of Common Ferns.* New York: G. P. Putnam's Sons, 1928.

Evers, Robert A., and Link, Roger P. *Poisonous Plants of the Midwest and their Effect on Livestock.* Urbana: University of Illinois Press, 1972.

Firth, Grace. *A Natural Year.* Boston: G. K. Hall and Co., 1973.

Fernald, M. L.; Kinsey, A. C.; and Rollins, R. C. *Edible Wild Plants of Eastern North America.* New York: Harper and Row, 1958.

Gibbons, Euell. *Stalking the Healthful Herbs.* New York: David McKay, 1966.

Gibbons, Euell. *Stalking the Wild Asparagus.* New York: David McKay, 1962.

Hall, Alan. *The Wild Food Trail Guide.* New York: Holt, Rinehart and Winston, 1973.

Hardin, James W., and Arena, Jay M., M. D. *Human Poisoning from Native and Cultivated Plants.* Durham, N. C.: Duke University Press, 1974.

Harris, Ben Charles. *Eat the Weeds*. Barre, Mass.: Barre Publishers, 1968.

Kimball, Yeffe, and Anderson, Jean. *The Art of American Indian Cooking*. Garden City, N. Y.: Doubleday, 1965.

Klein, Isabelle H. *Wild Flowers of Ohio and Adjacent States*. Cleveland: The Press of Case Western Reserve University, 1970.

Komaiko, Jean, and Schaeffer, Norma. *Doing the Dunes*. Beverly Shores, Ind.: Dune Enterprises, 1973.

Lindsey, Alton A., editor. *Natural Features of Indiana*. Indianapolis: Indiana Academy of Science, Indiana State Library, 1966.

Lindsey, A. A.; Schmelz, D. V.; and Nichols, S. A. *Natural Areas in Indiana and their Preservation*. Lafayette: Indiana Natural Areas Survey, Department of Biological Science, Purdue University, 1969.

Martin, Alexander C. *Weeds*. New York: Golden Press, 1972.

Matthews, F. Schuyler. *Field Book of American Wildflowers*. Revised by Norman Taylor. New York: G. P. Putnam's Sons, 1955.

Medsger, Oliver Perry. *Edible Wild Plants*. New York: Macmillan, 1939.

Miller, Orson K., Jr. *Mushrooms of North America*. New York: E. P. Dutton and Company, 1972.

Mother Earth News. Hendersonville, N. C.: The Mother Earth News, Inc., 1971–1974. Volumes 7–30.

Niethammer, Carolyn. *American Indian Food and Lore*. New York: Collier-Macmillan, 1974.

Peattie, Donald Culross. *Flora of the Indiana Dunes*. Chicago: Field Museum of Natural History, 1930.

Peterson, Roger T., and McKenny, Margaret. *A Field Guide to Wildflowers of Northeastern and North-Central North America*. Boston: Houghton Mifflin Co., 1968.

Petrides, George A. *A Field Guide to Trees and Shrubs*. Boston: Houghton Mifflin Co., 1972.

Pokagon, Chief. *Queen of the Woods*. Hartford, Mich.: C. H. Engle Publisher, 1901.

Smith, Alexander H. *The Mushroom Hunter's Field Guide*. Ann Arbor: University of Michigan Press, 1969.

Smith, Huron K. *Ethnobotany of the Forest Pottawatomi Indians*. Milwaukee: Bulletin of the Public Museum of the City of Milwaukee, 1933. Vol. 7, No. l, pp.1–230.

Weiner, Michael A. *Earth Medicine—Earth Foods*. New York: Macmillan Co., 1972.

INDEX

Nov. 1979